P9-DCL-229

Twayne's United States Authors Series

Sylvia E. Bowman, *Editor*

INDIANA UNIVERSITY

George Ripley

TUSAS 281

Geo. Ripley

GEORGE RIPLEY

By HENRY L. GOLEMBA

Wayne State University

TWAYNE PUBLISHERS
A DIVISION OF G. K. HALL & CO., BOSTON

First Printing

Library of Congress Cataloging in Publication Data

Golemba, Henry L
George Ripley.

(Twayne's United States authors series ;
TUSAS 281)
Bibliography: p. 164-69.
Includes index.
1. Ripley, George, 1802-1880. 2. Litterateurs
— United States — Biography.
PS2713.G6 809 [B] 76-41768
ISBN 0-8057-7181-6

MANUFACTURED IN THE UNITED STATES OF AMERICA

For

Adine

Contents

About the Author

After receiving a bachelor's degree from Monteith College of Wayne State University in 1965, Henry L. Golemba taught in experimental programs at junior colleges in Warren, Michigan, and Fort Worth, Texas, before pursuing graduate work at the University of Washington in Seattle where he received a doctorate degree in 1971. His graduate studies focused on Transcendentalism, and the resultant dissertation on Margaret Fuller's literary criticism and esthetic theory has been accepted for publication. While doing research on Margaret Fuller, Dr. Golemba first became interested in George Ripley as a paramount force in nineteenth-century American culture. Currently, Dr. Golemba is assistant professor of American literature at Wayne State University in Detroit, and he has published articles on John Steinbeck, Walt Whitman, Edgar Allan Poe, Caroline Kirkland, Herman Melville, and Jacob Bronowski in such magazines as *Modern Fiction Studies*, *The American Transcendental Quarterly*, *Criticism*, *Midwestern Miscellany*, *Studies in the Novel*, and *Among Friends*. Dr. Golemba has read papers before the Society for the Study of Midwestern Literature and the Modern Language Association on subjects ranging from science fiction to late nineteenth-century Realism. His current interest in the relationship between science and the arts has led him to write a novel about the future called *And by Confusion* and to investigate the impact of scientific theory upon early nineteenth-century writers, particularly Herman Melville and Edgar Allan Poe.

Preface

George Ripley, one of the more influential men of his era, left his mark on theology, politics, science, and literature. He was a radical thinker to theologians, a vigorous activist to conservative politicians, an articulate spokesman among Transcendentalists, and a steady supporter of burgeoning scientific, philosophical, and literary achievements. Nonetheless, the caprice of history has denied him a prominent place in the intellectual life of nineteenth-century America. The chief aims of this study are to understand the reasons for his esteem among his contemporaries and for his obscurity in the twentieth century. To achieve these objectives, it is necessary to clarify and assess as objectively as possible the significant thoughts of this man who for over fifty years was considered one of the preëminent intellectuals in America.

Three subsidiary goals are integral with this main objective. First, the issue of Transcendentalism needs further clarification. Its esthetics, varieties, and politics are matters that scholars continue to explicate. Since Ripley was the acknowledged leader of one mainstream of Transcendentalism — a current that included Theodore Parker, Orestes A. Brownson, John Sullivan Dwight, and James Freeman Clarke — familiarity with Ripley's thoughts can reveal his importance in this movement both in its narrower and in its broader aspects. For those who see Transcendentalism as including more than Emersonianism, this study of Ripley should prove helpful.

Moreover, since Ripley's interests were so varied, his work is a rich source from which a fresh survey of nineteenth-century culture in America may be made. With thoughts and opinions on almost every major issue of his day, he ventured boldly into every field of intellectual battle. A controversial figure, he had important points to make about capitalism, Socialism, feminism, racism, education, and labor unions. Exploration of these diverse areas in which he moved so freely and confidently provides a newer and more accurate measure of Ripley's worth in relationship to his own times. As Emerson rightly said, a study of even part of Ripley's life would provide a "fine historiette of the age."

A further aim of this study is to rescue from obscurity the biography of Ripley and to demonstrate the validity of the Transcendental tenet that a man's words and deeds were of secondary importance to the quality of life he led. How Ripley fought his battles and how he endured sorrow and disappointment are a testament to his strength and optimism. Even at the nadir of his life when he was in deep financial straits, in grief over the loss of his wife, and in pain from illness and failing eyesight, he did not despair. A lesser man would have been broken, but Ripley in strength and optimism proclaimed, "I am still at the top of the universe." His biography reveals him as a vital, forceful personality against a background of many powerful and engrossing figures.

To achieve these four principal aims, I have had to adopt specific approaches. In the first place, Ripley's biography and work are inseparable. His thought was much influenced by major events ranging from presidential campaigns to scientific discoveries. His firsthand experience with the Panic of 1837 would not allow him to be so confidently self-contained as Emerson. Consequently, my study of his life and work proceeds chronologically since each major event in his life wrought nuances of change in his thought and actions. Collaterally, my study of his life is organic, not mechanical. I see his career as all of one piece. I follow ideas Ripley expressed in 1830 to see what modifications they underwent in the next fifty years of his life. In this regard, my study differs greatly from that of others, for, while previous critics nearly omit mention of *The Harbinger* and treat Ripley's New York years as a sort of appendix to his career, I see these late phases of his life as an organic growth — even as a culmination.

One final approach deserves mention. No study of Ripley would be complete without attention to Brook Farm, the most famous experiment in practical Transcendentalism after Walden. This experiment is the hub of Ripley's biography: his thoughts and actions prior to 1841 look forward to it, and his career after 1847 was deeply influenced by it. This book divides Brook Farm into two distinct phases — Transcendental and Socialistic — and gives a concise description of them. More than other studies, this one probes the goals and motivations for Brook Farm more specifically and systematically. In doing so, it argues that Brook Farm is not an anomaly, but rather an integral element of the whole of Ripley's lifelong philosophy.

Preface

Throughout my research and study I have benefited from the cooperation and generosity of many. Henry W. Sams and Charles Crowe were kind enough to share their insights with me through correspondence. Sylvia Bowman, Samuel Golden, and Joel Myerson provided valuable advice in composing this manuscript. William Harrison, director, Fruitlands Museum, supplied important details and letters. The staffs of the Houghton Library, the Boston Public Library, and the Massachusetts Historical Society allowed me full use of their rare holdings and gave me permission to quote from Ripley's letters and manuscripts. A Faculty Research Award from Wayne State University gave me time to conduct a large part of the research.

HENRY GOLEMBA

Wayne State University

Chronology

1802 George Ripley born, October 3, in Greenfield, Massachusetts.
1819 Meets Ezra Ripley in June; arrives at Harvard University in September.
1823 Graduates from Harvard; enters Cambridge Divinity School.
1826 Is ordained pastor over Purchase Street Church, Boston, on November 8.
1827 Marries Sophia Willard Dana, August 22.
1830 Begins controversial essays for *The Christian Examiner.*
1836 Starts Transcendental Club; publishes *Discourses on Religion.*
1838 Visits communes; publishes *Specimens of Foreign Standard Literature.*
1839 Debates in Norton-Ripley controversy.
1840 Edits *The Dial*; quits ministry in May.
1841 Founds Brook Farm (April 1) which lasts until September, 1847.
1845 Begins *The Harbinger* which is discontinued in 1849.
1848 Sophia's religious crisis.
1849 Writes for *The New York Tribune* and other periodicals.
1850 Founds *Harper's Magazine.*
1852 Publishes *Handbook on Literature and the Fine Arts.*
1861 Sophia dies.
1862 Publishes *The American Encyclopaedia.*
1865 Marries Louisa Augusta Schlossberger on October 18.
1866 Visits Europe, mainly Germany, to cover the Austro-Prussian War.
1869 Revisits Europe; organizes the National Institute of Literature, Art, and Science.
1880 Dies on July 4 in New York.

CHAPTER 1

Youth and Education

I *Greenfield*

GEORGE Ripley's ancestors landed in the new World not long after the *Mayflower*. Seeking the New Zion, they settled at Hingham, Massachusetts, where they stayed for one hundred forty years. During Revolutionary years, one Ripley, an iron-willed man named Jerome, decided to risk a move to Boston in hopes of gaining riches. New England at large was tilting away from the values of the Puritans to those of Ben Franklin's Poor Richard, and Jerome hoped Boston would allow an honest if not a compassionate man like him to rise. But Boston, while long on gentility, was short on opportunity.

Believing the fields might be greener along the frontier of Western Massachusetts, Jerome moved to the Berkshire Mountain region in 1789. There, in Greenfield, his dream came true. He bought an eight-acre lot and established in 1791 a public house which later became a general store and tavern. By 1800, he was one of the wealthiest men in the town and was esteemed as a political, religious, and social leader. By the time of his ninth child's birth on October 3, 1802 — a child he named George — Jerome had risen from indigent newcomer to community pillar.

Born with his back to the Berkshires, George Ripley was clearly a child of place. Western Massachusetts encouraged and required individuality, independence, and ruggedness — a ruggedness to match the mountains. To outsiders, the region was noted primarily for two group actions. In the 1780's Daniel Shays, believing that the government had betrayed the Revolutionary principles for which he had bled, led one thousand two hundred dispossessed farmers in an attempt to stage a second revolution. The Shakers of the same region were likewise dissatisfied with society, but they resorted to plowshares and psalmistry instead of swords. Through peaceful communal living, not physical violence, they hoped to create a spiritual kingdom on earth.[1]

Both of these radical responses to society influenced Ripley in his adult life. Working in the tradition of Shays, he would have no qualms about challenging the Establishment and about striving to retool its machinery. Like the Shakers, he sought to do so in order to achieve the loftiest principles of truth, harmony, peace, and spiritual rejuvenation. The Shaker side might urge him to retreat from society, but the Shays part would demand direct action. Both sides emphasized group effort, criticism of society's ills, and faith in a better life.

These values were to become hallmarks of the mature George Ripley, but his character as a youth was much otherwise. From his birth in 1802 when a plague killed many, including George's brother, until 1819 when he left for Harvard University under forced march, George grew up in a household overflowing with motherly and sisterly care. His nearest brother, thirteen years his senior, was well on his way to becoming a lawyer and a banker. His autocratic father was busy making money, filling various political offices, and forcing his will in church affairs. His mother, Sarah Franklin Ripley, a kinswoman of Benjamin Franklin, was conservative in every respect. She and George's closest sisters, all older than he, trained George in the rules of decorum, taught him his lessons, filled him with orthodox Calvinist principles, and only in the matter of religious indoctrination was Jerome's will balked. As a man who had risen from rags to riches by his own power, he had little sympathy for the concept of an angry God.[2] But he had so many affairs to attend to that he decided to leave George's upbringing entirely to his wife and daughters. He would step in only when crucial decisions such as the choice of college had to be made.

In such surroundings, George grew to become what Mark Twain would call a "good little boy," an eminently tractable child who learned all he was taught and did all he was told. A handsome youth, smart and scholarly, he must have detected an odd disparity between what he was taught and what he saw. He was informed that Greenfield was a close-knit community which esteemed order, unity, and harmony; but this Puritan village already showed signs of disintegration. Controversies raged in 1809 over Federalist and Democratic presidential candidates. In 1814, when George was twelve years old, the church leaders, his father among them, condemned a woman to social ostracism for misdemeanors such as not attending church on the Sabbath. In 1816, Jerome, discontented with the fiery Puritanism of the First Congregational Church, sought to gerrymander the tiny town in order to establish a second church that sponsored more moderate Calvinist views.

An intelligent youth, George must have been struck by the strange contrast between the way the town thought of itself and the way it actually was. Early in his life, he must have sensed the disjunction between the ideal and the real, between model conceptions and actual states. His later experiment with Brook Farm might be seen as an attempt to recapture the closeness of Greenfield without permitting its materialism, its petty rivalries, and its vicious intolerance. As to the town itself, Ripley as an adult visited Greenfield only to attend the death of a relative or the installation of a new minister.

All his life, Ripley was to show traits which were conditioned by his childhood. He appeared warm and cheerful to friends, but forbidding to strangers. He glowed with a sense of mission, but exercised genial toleration. He would lead, but never force. He was handy as a farmer or craftsman and knowledgeable as a scholar. He would sorrow over miseries, the greatest being the inability of man to achieve his ideals. He would always adhere to the principle of self-culture, seek the maximum development of the individual, search constantly for the best means to achieve this goal.

As the son of a prosperous and respectable Greenfield citizen, George was sent away to school to prepare for college. At Mr. Huntington's academy at Hadley, Massachusetts, he excelled particularly in literature and mathematics. Although clearly a superb scholar, he expressed doubts while at Hadley about his ability to cope both intellectually and morally with college. On July 10, 1818, he wrote to his father, ". . . I feel emboldened to make the request that, if consistent with your inclinations and plans, I may receive an education at Yale rather than Cambridge."[3] Although Harvard was better in literature, Yale excelled in the "solid subjects." Most of all, "the temptations incident to a college" seemed fewer at Yale than at Cambridge.

This request did not at all fit into Jerome's inclinations and plans. A shrewd forecaster of business trends, he was no less perceptive in seeing that the old-style Puritanism with which his wife had filled young George's head could not keep step with the changing times. Because Yale was too conservative and because George would be sent to Harvard in spite of his fears, George started the five-day stagecoach ride to Cambridge in June, 1819. His anxieties en route over leaving a rural village to begin life at mighty Harvard across the river from the cultural hub of the universe — Boston — must have been prodigious.

To cushion the shock, he was to stay for three months in Lincoln, Massachusetts, with a relative named Ezra Ripley, a minister with Unitarian leanings who had married the aunt of Ralph Waldo Emerson. Ezra was an odd sort of minister who, as Emerson says, had a strong "partiality for ladies" and was "much addicted to kissing."[4] He was a "Modern Israelite" who was courtly, hospitable, public spirited, and who believed in the efficacy of prayers, especially those that affected the weather. His text was the Old Testament, but his model was Ben Franklin.

George's emotional state at meeting his relative was a combination of bafflement and dread. Ezra's complex conservative-liberal, Israelite-Unitarian, courtier-Calvinist tendencies confused George. The presence of several young Harvard men who were also staying at Ezra's house, preparing for their examinations in the fall, conversing fluently on John Locke, William Paley, David Hume, and Deuteronomy, filled George with greater apprehension about embarking upon this new phase of his life. In his young eyes, Harvard loomed as an even larger challenge because of the accomplishments of these young scholars. George learned much in this novel and stimulating atmosphere. After spending three months at Ezra Ripley's, when in September the time came for George to leave for Cambridge, he did so with heightened anticipation in addition to his persistent apprehension.

II *Harvard*

When George arrived on Harvard's campus, its ambience thoroughly surprised him. At Ezra's house, he had received intimations that Cambridge scholars were a peculiar breed; but reality outstripped his imaginings; the scholars he met were not at all sedate. In fact, they caroused at the local tavern, gambled, thumbed their noses at authority, and generally exceeded in every way Ezra's eccentricities. The moral temptations George had feared were all here in force. On the other hand, tutors were sharp, knowledgeable to an extent that would shame Mr. Huntington. Moreover, their particular form of knowledge was unintimidating to Ripley. It was as heavy and massive as the college's architecture, for the professors emphasized rote memorization over imagination so much that William Austin called Harvard "the death of genius." George knew he could cope with this academic regimen since all it required was perseverance, concentration, and a modicum of native intelligence. Since his nature was conditioned to seriousness and sobriety, neither need he fear engaging in peccadillos. As early as October of his freshman year, he could comfortably inform his mother that he had every confidence that he could succeed at Harvard and become a "correct and accurate scholar."[5]

Changes were imminent. That same year William Ellery Channing's sermon at the ordination of Jared Sparks made a clear break between Calvinism and Unitarianism and planted the seeds for the growth of Transcendentalism. George Ticknor and Edward Everett, who had returned from Germany, were pushing for liberal reform in curriculum and college life. Ripley came to Harvard to find a stable environment; but, after his first year, he was to be stimulated by intellectual ferment and by student demands.

Before Ripley's sophomore year, he met his first crisis. When students, wearied of the appalling food, staged a minor uprising under the leadership of John Robinson, Ripley attempted at first to avoid the disturbance. However, he soon decided he had to attempt to reconcile the students and administration. The students, as might be expected, disliked his attempts at conciliation and awarded him the verse:

> Then R-PL-Y the pious, as fickle as the wind,
> For nine times an hour he changes his mind,
> With pick-nosed W--d, who likewise did appear
> And W-i-t the old hard head who brought up the rear.[6]

In trying to be a good little boy and do the right thing, Ripley was whipped with his peers' displeasure. By the time of the "great rebellion" of May 2, 1823, a larger uprising over the same grievances, Ripley had learned his lesson. Although he still stood with the friends of order instead of with the fiends of reform, he remained quiet and let the contesting parties battle. He once again felt so alienated that he contemplated going away to conservative

Andover Academy for graduate studies rather than continuing at Harvard.

Other problems plagued Ripley as an undergraduate. Perhaps one reason he did not side with the campus rebels was that their food reforms seemed minor to him when compared to the voracious spirit of personal rivalry that Harvard trained into them. On May 15, 1820, Ripley complained to his mother that "the competition for scholarship has been zealous and energetic, and each party jealous of the other strives to win the prize." While by no means a strident condemnation of cutthroat competition, this letter shows Ripley's first inkling that the way of things was amiss. Later in his life, Ripley would become famous for opposing such overly competitive zeal.

These two rebellions also served to make Ripley more painfully conscious of his dependence upon his father. Since Jerome was quite prosperous, Ripley should have had funds readily available; but his letters exude anxieties over his educational costs. His schooling certainly was not the financial cross he presented it as being, and his worries must have been born of a longing for independence as well as from the urge for "emancipation from the restraints of college and power to take a more active and more conspicuous part in the great theatre of life."[7] In the winter of 1823, Ripley tried to ease his financial obligation and dodged a visit home by teaching school in Fitchburg where he was regaled as the Harvard scholar.

Ripley also experienced intellectual changes. On October 12, 1822, he began to keep a commonplace book on the plan recommended by John Locke, the principal philosopher whom Ripley later assailed as the apostle of materialism. Even this early, Ripley knew that not Locke but his disciples were responsible for excluding intuition as a useful means of knowledge. He referred to a section in the *Essay Concerning Human Understanding* which says:

> *Reason* is Natural *Revelation*, whereby the eternal Father of Right and Fountain of all knowledge communicates to mankind that portion of truth which he has laid within the reach of their natural faculties; *revelation* is natural *reason* enlarged by a new set of discoveries communicated by God immediately, which reason vouches the truth of, by the testimony and proofs it gives that They come from God. So that he that takes away *reason* to make way for *revelation* puts out the light of both, and does much . . . the same, as if he would persuade a man to put out his eyes the better to receive the remote light of an invisible star by a telescope.[8]

This entry in Ripley's commonplace book indicates that, fourteen years before Emerson published *Nature,* Ripley grappled with the conflict between reason and intuition which was to become the crux of Transcendental argument. This dialogue between reason and revelation (or intuition) was one to which Ripley would bend his ear all his life. His respect for reason prevented him from accepting the ethereal speculations of Bronson Alcott and Emanuel Swedenborg, and his belief in the power of intuition allowed him to make great leaps beyond the limits of logic.

In the privacy of his journal Ripley also came to grips with his own ambitions and goals. Among his earliest entries is a quotation from a letter of Milton's wherein the drudgery of scholastic pursuits is exonerated: "A desire of honour and of repute and of immortal fame, seated in the breast of every true scholar." Ripley's Puritanical upbringing warned him that pride was the chief of the Seven Deadly Sins, but Ripley solved this problem through an acute and realistic philosophy.

> We must regard the moral constitution of man as complex — made up of various parts and principles. Now there are certain principles the gratification of which imparts happiness to ourselves and not to others; there are certain other principles the gratification of which imparts happiness to others as well as ourselves; the man who acts upon the first set of principles I should call a selfish man; the man who acts upon the latter is a benevolent man. It appears from this that it is not necessary . . . that all regards to self be excluded. The duty of man is not to avoid his own happiness but to find it in the pursuit of those objects which have reference to others and do not terminate in himself.[9]

Neither a proponent of rampant selfishness nor pious self-abnegation — he would always be contemptuous of the former and suspicious of the latter — Ripley, while remaining aloof from campus disturbances, uttered the first word in his lifelong occupation with social reform and betterment — an activity which, like Thoreau's concept of civil disobedience, was not a right nor a privilege but a duty and an obligation. He reiterated this new calling by vowing to remain faithful to "those great principles of moral reformability . . . which though often dimmed by ignorance and vice are never thoroughly eradicated from the human heart."[10]

Although sequestered in his study, Ripley was not dormant as an undergraduate. His mind was growing, accumulating information, and pinpointing areas — notably the philosophical problem of reason and intuition and the social aims of reform — which would occupy him for a lifetime. He surpassed his greatest academic expectation by graduating at the top of his class with a brace of Bowdoin Prizes to his credit. But he had had enough of Harvard and wanted to go to Andover. His father, consistent though not considerate in behavior, foiled that wish. Ripley was to spend three more years in Cambridge.

III *Divinity School*

Ripley's graduation was a true commencement in that 1823 marked new directions in his mind and personality. His most notable personal achievement was to gain some feeling of independence. The Fitchburg teaching experience was a help, for Ripley at last was accorded respect. The freer atmosphere of graduate school let him feel that he was more his own man. He gathered about him a small circle of friends, let his inherent good humor and penchant for puns have full rein, and shed the opprobrious label of "Ripley the pious." His feeling of freedom and independence prevailed so completely that in his last year at Divinity School he began to court Sophia Willard Dana, an independent girl of genteel background whose charm exceeded her beauty. They became engaged secretly — secretly, at least, to father Jerome.

This is not to say that Ripley was becoming a flippant socialite. His Puritanical roots were still firm enough to prevent him from indulging in frivolity. He was becoming known as a good sort by his classmates and mentors, but, as he told his mother, "Much as I love company and gayety, I do love study and retirement best."[11] In the privacy of his study Ripley was busy "perfecting religion," part of which involved analyzing German writers — he had begun his first German studies in September, 1823 — and playing their near-mystical insights against the required readings of English empiricist philosophers, most notably John Locke and William Paley.

In perfecting his religion, Ripley began to cast off the last traces of orthodox Calvinism and take on the trappings of Unitarianism. He came to admire Unitarians and relinquished the bias that, because they dared smile, they lacked seriousness: "I had some prejudice against many of its members, who, destitute of austerity, I had thought to be deficient in the spirit of religion. But if a more intimate acquaintance has enabled me to judge rightly, the depth and purity of their religious feelings . . . is enough to humble and shame those who have . . . pretended to superior sanctity."[12] Another attraction for Ripley to this new religion was that the Unitarians were underdogs; were called infidels by some, heretics by others; and were persistently blasted from all quarters, as he said, by "the busy spirit of misrepresentation and detraction."

A lay Freudian might add that another attraction could be that, by becoming an Unitarian, Ripley could at last escape his father's psychological domination. He had tried to remain true to his mother's orthodoxy first by preferring Yale over Harvard and later by requesting to be sent to Andover instead of Cambridge, but in both cases his father had thwarted his will. He failed to escape his father by keeping to the theological right; Unitarianism with which he had staunchly allied himself by January 26, 1824,[13] was a way to leave his father behind by surpassing his religious liberalism. A Unitarian church was not established in Greenfield until 1825, and Jerome did not join until several years after.

The predominant reason for Ripley's conversion was that Unitarianism seemed the best means for achieving an understanding of God. Puritanism with its hell-fire and brimstone ceased to be an effective method of awakening religious passion. Ripley's associations with orthodoxy were "days of mistaken zeal for religion," and they caused him to express "crude, hasty sentiments concerning things of which [he] was utterly ignorant."[14] Fear and threats were no longer effective in awakening the soul; instead, Ripley argued, man could trust in reason which, coupled with faith, could illuminate the farthest reaches of truth and goodness, "the dearest hopes and the most sacred emotions." In place of the blind faith and the unreliable enthusiasm of Calvinism, Unitarianism promised a clear and logical exposition of religion.

This falling away from orthodoxy caused no slight stir in Greenfield. A childhood sweetheart wrote to Ripley to warn him that he should consider his actions since they were the talk of the town. Ripley stridently replied, "The opinion of the world is but a puff of empty air. Let the world say what it pleases; truth and truth unpopular and odious, — aye and that which is stigmatized as heresy and sin — must be sought and professed by the consistent Christian."[15] This untempered contempt for social opinion when it interfered with what Ripley conceived to be the truth later became his hallmark as a reformer and critic. This letter marks his first unqualified and unequivocal declaration of intellectual independence.

If the good citizens of Greenfield had known how far Ripley was moving away from them, their idle gossip would have turned to gasps of shock; for Ripley was developing one of the most extreme versions of the most extreme form of Protestantism. Indeed, he saw himself as a Christian independent of any branch of religion, a believer in principles above every sect and theological system. His principal credo became the biblical injunction, "Beloved, let us love one another, for love is of God, and he that dwelleth in God and He in him."[16] With this motto as a fundamental belief, rites, rituals, and ceremonies became mere frills. Ironically, Ripley traveled full circle back to a purified Puritanism in seeking for the "original purity" of Jesus' teachings. Unitarianism, far from being an end in itself, was a useful corkscrew for getting at the sacramental wine, one far more useful than the heavy and hot hammer of Calvinism.

Ripley clarified his alliance with the most radical wing of liberal Christianity by adopting Levi Frisbie, the Alford Professor of Natural Religion, as his mentor. Frisbie, who had been installed two years before Ripley entered Harvard, made a double impression. Immersed in the Scottish common sense psychology, Frisbie, in contrast to the sensualists who held that all values and concepts were the product of the senses in interaction with reality, insisted on the autonomy of morality and argued that "right" transcended environmental conditioning. Moreover, he asserted that, since human nature was made in God's image, it was a reliable means for ascertaining religious truth independent of proof by miracles and by logic. Frisbie thereby provided the kernel of thought that Ripley would develop into his special brand of Transcendentalism which emphasized intuition and a collective verification of virtue while scorning traditional authority, rapacious selfishness, and the exclusive appeal to mundane experience.

If the town of Greenfield were unaware of the imminent extremism of Ripley's thought, so, evidently, were his professors. They saw this intelligent, scholarly, studious individual as their great hope for preserving and promoting this new sect, Unitarianism. At Ripley's ordination, the greatest Unitarian names presided, including John Thornton Kirkland, president of Harvard, and Henry Ware, one of the influential forces who would later side with Andrews Norton's conservative position in the famous Norton-Ripley controversy of 1839-40. Little did these men know that they had nurtured a viper, that the man in whom they placed such confidence would soon shake the institution of Unitarianism to its foundations and change it irrevocably.

If the Harvard luminaries were unaware of what lightning Ripley would shake out, so probably was Ripley himself. He was still by nature a good little boy. He had studied the prescribed curriculum, had questioned as he was told to question, had listened with a keen mind to the ideas proffered by the Harvard dons, and had moved to conclusions that to him seemed only reasonable and sensible. The professors were soon to be placed in the awkward position of parents criticized by their child for not abiding by the very principles they had advocated. In installing Ripley on November 8, 1826, in a Unitarian society formed expressly for him, neither they nor Ripley foresaw the tremendous challenges he would raise.

Later in life, while working for the *New York Tribune,* Ripley reviewed a biography for no clear reason except that the subject, Professor B. B. Edwards, was an example of what Ripley might have become under different circumstances. Edwards was born in the same year as Ripley near Ripley's school town (Hadley, Massachusetts), was a serious and religious Puritan child who grew up to be a good man like Ripley, was an editor and antislavery advocate like Ripley, but was obscure and unknown. His major failing was that "He has thrown no new light in questions of practical or speculative interest by the force of original thought."[17] Possibly Ripley saw Edwards as the uninfluential man Ripley might have been had he succeeded in finding "some retired literary position" instead of challenging nineteenth-century America on social, political, religious, and intellectual fronts.

CHAPTER 2

From Minister to Militant

I *The Pulpit*

RIPLEY mounted the pulpit of his new church made up of wealthy, middle-class Bostonians with great expectations. He hoped to shed light upon the world; and the Purchase Street Church located across from the site of the Boston Tea Party was to be his lamp. He served the congregation for nearly fifteen years from November 8, 1826, to March 28, 1841. In the first five years he concentrated on enlightening his flock and defending Unitarianism which was then much under attack. From 1832 to 1836, he developed Unitarianism to such an extreme that the more conservative members raised cries of heresy; Ripley was baffled that his congregation could not follow him in his discoveries; and he was shocked when Andrews Norton attacked him for infidelity in 1836. In the last five years of his ministry Ripley almost gave up on his congregation. He served up uncontroversial sermons and saved his profound and radical ideas for outside lectures and periodicals.

At first, his hopes for the parish seemed justified. On November 26, 1826, he wrote to his mother: "I am . . . better pleased than I at first expected. . . . My people are particularly kind to me, and seem disposed to receive all my attempts to move them with real indulgence."[1] He immediately wrote a constitution for the Association for Mutual Religious Improvement which emphasized study and knowledge as well as charity work, and members of the congregation were indulgent enough to sign. He entertained all the causes that a respectable minister should promote, including the Massachusetts Evangelical Missionary Society of which he was state secretary and the Council of Massachusetts Temperance Society. His flock grew so accustomed to Ripley's reform interests that, when he later championed antislavery at a time when other like-minded ministers found themselves expelled from the pulpit, hardly a ripple was caused.[2]

On a broader scale, Ripley was fulfilling his role as the great hope of Unitarianism by preaching sermons and by publishing tracts about the major differences between Unitarianism and other Christian sects. In the tract "A Letter to a Trinitarian Friend," he argued that the doctrine of the trinity does not survive reason and biblical scholarship, and that one must therefore either become a Unitarian and profess the truth or be a Catholic and wallow in the glorification of mystery. In his sermon "The Divinity of Jesus Christ," he was consummately orthodox in asserting that Jesus was not man and not God but an intermediary whose wisdom "was not his own, but was given him by his Father." Not an inkling of Ripley's imminent Transcendentalism is present in these early sermons, nor is there any premonition of his later battle with other Unitarians over the question of the reliability of Scripture and the importance of miracles. He says of Unitarian conclusions, "our sentiments . . . are derived, not from the instructions of human reason, but from the light of sacred scriptures."[3]

In uttering these highly orthodox claims, Ripley was obviously carried away with the defense of besieged Unitarianism. He felt his cause was good; for, as he said in 1840 upon leaving the ministry, "In 1826, the Unitarian controversy was in the ascendant; it excited general interest; questions of dogmatic theology were in every mouth . . . for the first time, religion became a subject of vast and solemn import to their souls. . . . That was a good state of things. It promised well for the future. It awakened the brightest hopes in regard to the practical influence of religion in the community."[4]

The impact Unitarianism had on the Purchase Street Church did not fulfill Ripley's hopes. As early as February 4, 1827, he recorded that the congregation was so uninspiring that a preacher ran the risk of falling into a dead palsy, "performing his sacred function with little more emotion than he would tend the boiler of a steam engine."[5] About two years later, he blamed Unitarianism's emphasis on rational sermons for the lack of success he was having with the Purchase Street Church. A Calvinist preacher could conjure up a vision of a sulphurous hell or a blissful heaven to urge his people on, but a Unitarian minister desired to produce a gradual and universal improvement of character and so adhered to principles and concepts that lacked objective correlatives. The Calvinist thus had the advantage, "just as it is easy to excite a populace to enthusiasm in favor of a man or party, but hard to make them good patriots."[6] As early as 1829, Ripley felt, therefore, the need for some concrete, living model to inspire his people to discussion if not to action; in ten years time, he would develop Brook Farm as just such an example.

In the late 1830's, Ripley's dismay with his congregation grew stronger and peaked during the Panic of 1837, an economic disaster of such magnitude that it rivals the Great Depression of the 1930's.[7] The economic system had exhibited its first dramatic failure, and everywhere Ripley beheld unemployment, starvation, and, worst of all, degradation. His role as minister was to reaffirm the divine nature of man, but the economic system mocked his every word and insisted on self-seeking, status-climbing, and also the worship of Mammon. Meanwhile, his congregation piously agreed with his sermons, but their only active efforts were to lament the invasion of riffraff into their community and the decline of Sunday contributions. At the close of his ministry, Ripley cited this apathy as one of his major reasons for leaving:

> The great fact of human equality before God is not one to let the heart remain cold; it is not a new speculative abstraction; it is something more than a watchword for a political party to gain power with and then do nothing to carry it into practical operation; it is a deep and solemn, vital truth, written by the Almighty in the laws of our being. . . . Blame me for it if you will, but I cannot behold the degradation, the ignorance, the poverty, the vice, the ruin of the soul which is everywhere displayed . . . in our own city while men look on without a shudder. I cannot witness the glaring inequalities of conditions, the hollow pretensions of pride, the scornful apathy with which many urge the prostration of man, the burning zeal with which they run the race of selfish competition with no thought for the elevation of their brethren. . . .[8]

The specter of economic privation had walked right into Purchase Street Church and spat on Ripley's text. This messenger of reality scoffed at every Transcendental word, insinuated that liberal Christianity and capitalism were irreconcilable, and prevented Ripley from desiring the self-contained form of Transcendentalism that Emerson espoused.

Consequently, Ripley felt the need in 1840 for missionary fervor more greatly than ever before, but he believed that the church on the corner of Purchase and Pearl streets could not kindle and spread his fire. In July, he asked to be relieved; but the proprietors looked upon his proposal with horror for they felt that Ripley's resignation would cost the already declining church some of its most respectable members. That they based their decision on church attendance and not on Christian ideals only proved to Ripley how little they had heeded his sermons.[9] On the first of October he tried to force their hands by delivering an ultimatum: he would stay for a maximum of one year, but the church had to change in two major ways. First, the service must be simplified to the state of original Christianity when converted fishermen gathered on the shore to speak with Jesus; tithes were to be eliminated; all contributions would be voluntary; pews would no longer be awarded according to social rank; and the congregation would regard itself as "a band of brothers" whose minister would not exhort nor dictate but lead and encourage.

Second, the congregation's spirit also had to be revitalized. They must accept Ripley's brand of militant, reformatory Transcendentalism — one that would stand "For temperance, against vice, slavery of any kind, for the poor, universal peace, against war" — not necessarily by joining any reform association, but by rooting out the humanly fallible causes of sin, crime, and error which lurked wtihin each person's breast. "It should be the effort of every true man to abolish [vice] altogether, to banish the principles [animal passions] from which they proceed."[10] In short, Ripley challenged his flock to abandon pietistic liberalism in favor of a Transcendentalism which insisted upon the equality and essential divinity of mankind. By January 1, 1841, Ripley decided his church was not meeting the challenge and handed in his formal resignation. He delivered his Farewell Discourse on March 8, 1841, and preached his last sermon on March 28. This particular lamp had turned cold, but Ripley's fire still flamed bright. In April, 1841, he established Brook Farm as one more attempt at practical Transcendentalism.

II *Examining Christianity*

While Ripley failed to stimulate his flock to follow his ideals, he did succeed in exciting people outside his congregation. A series of ten articles for the *Christian Examiner* from 1830 to 1837 brought him into collision with some of the biggest names in Unitarianism. Through sermons delivered at other churches, he emerged as the leader of the radical wing of Unitarianism which came to be known as Transcendentalism. Ripley became the man who, as O. B. Frothingham has said, "was as influential as any in planting the seeds of the Transcendental philosophy in good soil, and in showing whither its principles tended."[11]

But Ripley's forceful leadership came about only after a long period of religious doubt and serious questioning of the validity of his convictions. On September 1, 1827, the same year that he expressed fear that the minister's soul might fall into a palsy, he recorded in the privacy of his journal that he was not at all as confident of his religion as he once had been. He concluded that "To decline active exertions for the religious improvement of man through any doubt with regard to the primary truths of religion would be as unwise as for . . . an engineer to decline the care of his machinery because he might be a convert to Berkeley's skeptical theories of the non-existence of matter." Even as late as April 6, 1832, Ripley's commonplace book reveals his brooding over the possibility that faith in God might be a negative concept — the antithesis of man's awareness of his own state. Man might believe in eternity because his own life is so transient; in infinity, because his life is but a speck; in the Almighty, because man is so weak; in an omniscient being, because man is grossly ignorant.

This dark underside of Transcendentalism is present in all Transcendental writings, but it is often overlooked because of the brightness of the Transcendentalist's optimistic claims. Through a serious and prolonged investigation of literature, philosophy, theology, and life, Ripley concluded that a person must accept either of two diametrically opposed views: one saw man as a depraved, savage, ignorant brute, as some Calvinists claimed; or a passive product of environment and a prisoner of his senses, as some eighteenth-century Empiricists imagined; the other view saw man as a god-like being with infinite potentiality and with a boundless future before him.

Either man must accept ignorance, vice, pettiness, and limitations as his true nature, or he must see these defects as errors and aberrations, not as true reflections of his innermost self. Consequently, in Ripley's first public Transcendental speech, "Jesus Christ, the Same, Yesterday, Today, and Forever," delivered at the ordination of Orestes Brownson on May 14, 1834, and repeated on request at least seven times before its publication in 1839, Ripley cites the search for immutable truths, the thirst for happiness, the vast capacity for love, and the other "deep wants of our nature [which] lead us to God" as betokening man's true condition; otherwise, "All is blank, and desolate, and lifeless, for to our darkened eye no God is present there."

Although this sermon was widely admired among Transcendentalists — Theodore Parker even paid it the most sincere form of flattery by imitating it in "The Transient and Permanent in Christianity"[12] — the speech is not so daring, so provocative, so well-reasoned, nor so well-documented as were Ripley's ten articles for the *Christian Examiner* which were written for a more informed audience of Unitarians. Most of the review articles were about men such as Joseph de Gérando, J. L. S. Vincent, the Swiss educator Johann Heinrich Pestalozzi, and German theologians like Johann Gottfried Herder, and Friedrich Daniel Schleiermacher, the founder of hermeneutics. Ripley was interested mainly in philosophers who were opposed to eighteenth-century rationalism, sensualism, and empiricism — the predominant emphases of Harvard's curriculum, a regimen of study that had stressed John Locke in philosophy and William Paley in theology.

The brand of Lockean sensualism that American Unitarians had developed involved three distinct steps. First, starting with the *tabula rasa* idea, Locke held that a man's mind at birth was a blank slate upon which experience was recorded. Hence all knowledge that came to a man did so through his five senses. Second, the processes of this gathering of knowledge were universal, a condition which offered the hope that the workings of the mind could someday be neatly calibrated and which opposed the belief that one could achieve mystical insight unaided by supernatural powers. Third, the biblical miracles, therefore, go beyond the natural human processes of gathering knowledge. They are supernatural and prove the existence of God and His participation in human affairs.

This last point was the most objectionable to Ripley. He questioned how man could know that the miracles performed by Jesus were divinely inspired while others — say those of Simon Magus and other magicians contemporary with Jesus — were sham. Since Locke had proved that rationality could not create nor authenticate Jesus' words and deeds, the proof must lie in another human faculty — one that Immanuel Kant called Pure Reason and others named Intuition. Some particle of divinity must be within each man that responds to God's truth but also sees Satan's tricks to be repulsive and magicians' antics to be supercilious.

Ripley objected to Unitarianism because it made man into a thinking machine and ignored his greatest gift — intuition. Moreover, Unitarianism tended to cleave man from God by insinuating that, although man was made in God's image, the child could not respond to the truth of his Father's voice without the benefit of a translator. Lastly, Unitarianism was undemocratic, for, while it asserted the universality of mental processes, it held that the untutored, untrained mind was incapable of knowing God unassisted by biblical scholars and ministers. This assertion struck Ripley as antithetical to original Christianity.

In making these objections to Unitarianism, Ripley felt he was condemning only one branch and not the entire sect.He did not reject Locke wholesale; indeed, he admired him greatly for explaining the workings of man's rationality. But he objected strenuously when Locke was used to argue against intuition, to deny man's essential divinity, or when Locke was pushed to the extreme of materialism and utilitarianism. William Channing, one of the prominent Unitarian divines, had proclaimed in 1819 that "God is within"; and Ripley was only taking him literally. Had not James Walker, the editor of the *Christian Examiner* and a former teacher of Ripley's, spoken out against the exclusive principle and insisted that a free intellectual inquiry, not dogmatism, was the hallmark of Unitarianism? Ripley saw himself as merely a leader of radical Unitarianism, not as an iconoclast who sought to demolish the sect. He felt that Locke was brilliant but limited; that his rationalism needed to be reconciled with intuition. Ripley sought an eclectic synthesis in which Unitarianism would provide a solution to the complexities of human nature.

In the first of Ripley's ten articles for the *Christian Examiner,* "De Gérando on Self-Education" (September, 1830), Ripley flaunted his originality and scholarship. Since these essays were designed to shape the views of his fellow learned ministers, he ranged across the full spectrum of philosophical opinion. He included eighteenth-century men like Ralph Cudworth, Henry More, Samuel Clarke, Joseph Butler, Richard Price, and John Smith who were known only in footnotes to other American intellectuals. He did so not merely to astound his fellow clergymen with his erudition

idea. In the article about Pestalozzi (January, 1832) he asserted that the principles of self-culture must be applied to society at large to insure the elevation of the entire species. The Schleiermacher article by Ripley gives this point more emphasis and insists upon a philosophy that satisfies the needs of a congregation of individuals. This satisfaction of needs involved style as well as content; and Ripley gave in "De Gérando's Self-Education" a positive description of what the new philosophy of Transcendentalism should do:

> We would see a more profound analysis of the soul, with its boundless capacities of suffering and enjoyment, its thirst for infinite good, its deep passions, its inexpressible wants, its lofty aspirations after the unseen and eternal. Man has been regarded too much as the creature of accidental circumstances, while the primary and indestructible laws of his being have been kept out of sight. We wish to see his whole nature clearly exhibited before us, with all the mysterious powers it involves. . . . We want a philosophy which recognizes the religious and immortal relations of the human race, — those holy and spiritual relations, which alone can explain the secret of our present existence, or cast any light on our future destiny — as well as the material ties, by which we are connected with the fleeting interests of our earthly condition, and bound for a few short years to our fellow men. We would have these relations not only recognized, but felt. . . . We do not wish them to be treated as subjects of cold, logical discussion . . . but to be held up in living colors, as everlasting realities, in which every human being has a deep and vital interest.[16]

To Ripley, Kant and other neo-Transcendentalists were right in their basic assumptions, but they tended to be either overly analytical like Kant and Cudworth or obscure like Coleridge and Herder. In 1830, Ripley was calling for an Emerson, a Thomas Carlyle, or a Walt Whitman to tell people of their divinity and god-like potential in such a way that they would feel the truth of these statements in every fiber of their being.

As long as Ripley restricted himself to popularizing European intellectuals, he was on safe ground and was even applauded as a bold and original scholar. To be interested in German and in French culture in America in the 1830's was to be considered culpable of moral laxity; but, if the interest were merely intellectual or theological it could then be tolerated since it was thought necessary to keep abreast of Continental developments. When Ripley responded to Francis Bowen's attack on Emerson's *Nature* and the Transcendental movement by citing Professor Ullman of the University of Halle, he was still playing within the rules of the growing controversy.[17]

But, when Ripley began to criticize Unitarian divines of the mother country, England, conservative Unitarians began to regard him as a threat. His attack on Sir James Mackintosh in the *Christian Examiner* for January, 1833, aroused their first suspicions. This English knight attempted purportedly to reconcile Hume's doctrine of utility with Joseph Butler's concept of the supremacy of conscience in order to produce a system of practical philanthropy, obviously a Ripleyan demand. But Ripley clearly indicated in this article that he would hold no truck with compromises and that eclecticism must not mean evasion of primary philosophical questions. Here was a man whom Ripley should have admired — or so the orthodox felt — but, instead, Ripley was going beyond even this supposed radical.

Wary Unitarian eyes watched this man who threatened to out-German the Germans; and, when Ripley in November, 1836, criticized one of the English Unitarian ministers, the dam burst. Reverend James Martineau, the brother of the famous social reformer Harriet Martineau, had published *The Rationale of Religious Enquiry* which Ripley reviewed, finding in it all those so-called liberal sentiments that he detested and lucklessly fought in his Purchase Street Church. Ripley focused on four main points which he had expressed before but not nearly so forcefully. He once more called for "an open and solemn marriage between faith and reason," and he finally established intuition as the fundamental human faculty. In "De Gérando" (1830), he had referred to the "test of inward conscience" in recognizing truth; in "Religion in France" (1831), he had spoken of a "secret conscience" as opposed to rationalism; in "Mackintosh" (1832), he had said that "intuitive perceptions are the foundations of moral science"; and in the article on Schleiermacher (March, 1836) he had reiterated the importance of the "primitive consciousness." But in this Martineau review, Ripley used the one word that would set him apart from his fellow Unitarians: he began to refer to intuition as "absolute." "The power of the soul, by which it gains the intuitive perception of spiritual truth, is the original inspiration that forms the common endowment of human nature. This, we maintain, is established by the testimony of the absolute and intuitive reason in man."[18]

Intuition thereby becomes the primary faculty for perceiving Divine Truths — brotherhood, equality, peace, harmony, the god-like potentiality of each human being — and the role of reason is to deduce the origin of these truths. Since "Divine Truths" are not created by man's own volition nor derived from any deductions of his understanding and since they do not spring from society and indeed are often countermanded by society, the authority of reason refers them to an external and supernatural source.

This new scheme in effect diminishes God's importance, for it makes a clear distinction between God and God's truths. Since man is capable of realizing God's word on his own, he has no need of God except to explain the origin of His word. God is "The Absolute Causality — the Inifinite Author of Truth and Good." Man, not God, is placed in the seat of judgment and can discover Truth and Goodness unaided by supernatural authority:

> Let us ascertain what is meant by the expression often used but little pondered — the Image of God in the Soul of Man. Let us determine whether our nature has any revelation of the Deity within itself; and, if so, analyze and describe it. If we there discover, as we firmly believe we shall, a criterion of truth by which we can pass judgment on the Spiritual and Infinite, we shall then be prepared to examine the claims of a Divine Revelation in history. [19]

God, in such statements, is not dead but merely irrelevant. He is to be thanked for making man in His image; and He is to be respected for having created Truth, Goodness, and Beauty. Otherwise, the Godhead is unimportant compared to the significance of the words He spoke. The purpose of man is to serve, not as the biographer of the Infinite Author, but as a critic of His works; man should focus not on the personality of God, but on His Word.

The issue on which this complicated philosophy centered was the question of miracles. Since Martineau held that the writers of the New Testament had not always been divinely inspired, careful scholarship was essential to determine which parts of the Scriptures were true. Ripley, however, believed man acknowledged the truths of the Bible not because they came from God but because they struck a responsive chord in man and seemed consonant with the image of God within man. As he had said in the Schleiermacher article, the nature of man authenticated the Bible. Therefore, as he had written in the second article on Herder (November, 1835), miracles were unimportant. They had certainly happened, but so had other miracles which were not of divine origin. How was man to sift true miracles from false ones except by the response of his inner being? The prophets believed they were divinely inspired, and so they were, but from within, not from without. To Ripley, supernatural inspiration was no more than a state of heightened natural inspiration and was to be judged by "its agreement with the primitive and absolute dictates of the absolute reason in man." [20]

Hence Ripley managed to combine the salient features of the three major religions in America. From the Puritans, he adopted Jonathan Edwards' concept of the will which maintains that there is an inherent element in man which aspires to godliness and that the power of words expressed in a moving way can do much to encourage this aspiration. Ripley's concept of God as an aloof Being uninvolved with man's affairs is similar to the belief of his ancestor Benjamin Franklin and of other Deists who conceived of a watchmaker God; however, Ripley believed that God was still active through His Word though not as a personality. Furthermore, Ripley retained the Unitarians' respect for reason, when it was used for or directed toward analyzing the workings of intuition. He reduced reason to a subservient function and focused it on the internal workings of psychology instead of man's external relationship with the universe through his senses.

The old-guard Unitarians like Henry Ware, who had presided at Ripley's ordination, and Andrews Norton, Ripley's former mentor at Harvard, saw Ripley not as a great synthesizer of American culture but as a heretical threat to the sect they had developed. This most brilliant student of the Class of '26 who was supposed to have been the great hope of Unitarianism now strove, in the eyes of the conservatives, to demolish all they had built. They had tolerated this viper nurtured in their bosoms long enough; the time had come to strike back, and strike back they forcefully did.

III *The Norton-Ripley Controversy*

During the years following Ripley's ordination, he had persisted in doing only what he had been trained to do — analyze Unitarianism, root out its weaknesses, and bring it more in line with its professed aims. Consequently, he believed he was merely fulfilling his role as the conscientious critic of his faith when he said of Martineau's Unitarianism:

> But what are our prevailing systems of theology? . . . It is hard to imagine a study more dry, more repulsive, more perplexing, and more totally unsatisfactory to a scientific mind than theology as presented in the works of by far the greater part of English writers on this subject. . . . It is no wonder that the heart is pulverized, that the freshness of life is exhausted under their influence. [21]

He knew James Martineau bore no grudge over this review. On December 29, 1826, two months after its publication, Ripley wrote to Thomas Carlyle saying that he and the Martineaus were "great friends." When he visited Martineau on his first trip to England in 1869, their meeting was full of cordiality and mutual respect. But Ripley also knew that some considered him a gadfly who was dangerous to the preservation of the sect. Andrews Norton, whom Sophia referred to as "the wicked Mr. Norton" in 1832 because of his bigotry, was particularly critical. But Ripley had not the least suspicion that Norton was so incensed that he would take the unprecedented step of slapping a fellow minister's wrists in public. On November 5, 1836, Norton published an open letter in the *Boston Daily Advertiser* condemning Ripley's review of Martineau's *Rationale.* He had tried to have the letter published in the *Christian Examiner,* but the editor, James Walker, declined — as much for Norton's sake as for Ripley's. No Unitarian minister had ever launched a personal attack on one of his colleagues, certainly not outside the domain of the professional or religious periodicals.

Besides the insult, Norton's action maddened Ripley; for Norton did not condescend to enumerate particulars but merely brandished generalities. Namely, Ripley was corrupting innocent souls with his heretical notions; and he would be wise to submit future manuscripts to more mature individuals, such as Norton, before publishing them. Ripley worked feverishly to prepare a reply, and it appeared in the *Advertiser* on November 9, 1836. Invoking the not-yet-established principle of academic freedom, he responded to Norton's censorship by telling him that Norton desired "to place shackles upon the press and to drown the voice of discussion by the cry of alarm."

Ripley also informed "Pope" Norton that the real difference between them was the matter of faith in man. Norton had been reared in the "school which was founded by Locke — the successor of Hobbes and the precursor of Condillac and Voltaire." Pushed to an extreme position by Norton's attack, Ripley asserted: "For that philosophy I have no respect. I believe it to be superficial, irreligious and false in its primary elements. The evils it brought upon humanity, by denying to the mind the power of perceiving spiritual truth are great and lamentable." Therefore, Ripley found it no surprise that "We live in an age of skepticism and vague thought on many of the most important subjects of belief; but for myself I am certain that no cold reserve, no coward fear, no spiritual despotism can remove or mitigate the evil. We want . . . discussion in which the love of truth shall be blended with a heartfelt trust in its power." [22]

Probably without realizing it, Ripley was severing himself from that wing of the Unitarian Church that Norton and other influential ministers represented. Norton had made no mention of the nature of man and the power of his will, but Ripley read his letter as representing the belief in the limitation of man and the pettiness of his will. Probably Ripley had in mind Orville Dewey's remarks asserting that, "Humanity . . . has too hard a lot . . . if God has not opened for it the fountains of revelation. . . . On the heart that is made to bear the weight of infinite interests, sinks the crushing burden of doubt and despondency, of fear and sorrow, of pain and death, without resources or relief, or comfort, or hope." [23] No longer was Ripley trading names with the conservatives by saying that Schleiermacher was more relevant than Paley; instead, he had brought the controversy to basics and pinpointed the fundamental difference between the radicals and the conservatives.

Norton, Dewey, and Ware believed that man was a weak creature whose only salvation was to throw himself on God's mercy and to trust in His (or His priests') wisdom; but Emerson, Brownson, and Ripley maintained that Christianity must be a living faith in which a man fires his soul to a point of heightened perception of God's truth. He could do so, the radicals maintained, unaided by priestly authority. In making this difference of opinion so fundamental, Ripley left no room for compromise. There were ways to accommodate Rationalism and mysticism, utilitarianism and spiritualism, sensational and intuitive faculties; but the schism was irreconcilable when the controversy centered on the very nature of the soul.

The causes of Norton's unprecedented actions are many and involve more than Ripley's single article on Martineau. In the first place, Norton felt an attack necessary in order to defend Unitarianism from charges of heresy made by more fundamental sects. In 1823, Samuel Miller, professor of theology at Princeton, had said, "It is evident that Unitarianism . . . consists of NOT BELIEVING." Ten years later a minister had reiterated in a Congregational publication that "The fire of unbelief has been the ruling spirit in your [Unitarian] system." Throughout the 1820's, Moses Stuart and Leonard Woods of Andover had lamented the "Germanizing" of Harvard.[24] In Norton's zeal to defend the propriety and orthodoxy of his religion, he grew rash and earned the epithet "Pope Norton" by invoking the "exclusive principle" by which those in authority claimed the privilege to censure the ideas of other members of their sect.[25]

Furthermore, Norton was alarmed, perhaps a bit panicked, by the rise of what was to become known as Transcendentalism. Besides being respected as a regular contributor to the *Examiner,* Ripley was gaining power in other circles. The *Christian Register* had asked him to be its editor for three months in 1833, and the *Boston Observer and Religious Intelligencer* had done likewise for six months in 1835. Moreover, the heretics were growing in number. Had not Brownson, whom Ripley ordained, published a sacrilegious review of Victor Cousin in the September, 1836, issue of the *Examiner?* Was not Emerson's *Nature,* which came out in the same month, clearly a pantheistic document?

But Brownson was unassailable because he respected the rules by cloaking his criticism of Unitarianism as a review of Continental philosophers. Emerson, too, was safe since he had left the ministry. In criticizing a fellow minister, however, Ripley had given the Transcendental screw a further twist and had carried the battle into the conservatives' own camp. If Ripley were so bold as to launch a major attack, Transcendentalism must now be a threat which called for extreme measures. Therefore, Norton sent his letter to the *Boston Advertiser.*

Instead of Norton's having the desired effect of shaming Ripley and of bringing him back into the fold, Ripley brazenly manned his position and, indeed, made the entrenchment deeper than ever. Realizing that Ripley could not be intimidated, Norton resorted to the use of personal influence. As co-editor of the *Examiner,* he threatened to resign if the periodical ever published another article by one of the radicals. The *Examiner* thus joined the ranks of all the other major periodicals in declining to publish Transcendental essays. But the fight was far from over. In two years the Norton-Ripley controversy would erupt into a fiery climax.

IV Discourses on Religion

Nine days after his reply to Norton, Ripley escalated the controversy from a fracas to a full-scale war, from an exchange of letters in the newspapers to a book-length barrage of six essays called *Discourses on the Philosophy of Religion.* In the *Advertiser* reply, Ripley had rebutted Norton's charge that he was not worthy of the name of Unitarian. In the *Discourses,* Ripley moved from sectarianism to principles; if his thoughts were not Unitarian, then Unitarianism was not true Christianity. As the subtitle of the *Discourses* implies ("Addressed to Doubters Who Wish to Believe"), Ripley divided Christians into two categories — Believers and Doubters; those who trust in the biblical maxim that man is made in God's image and is therefore divine, and those who deny this statement while falsely retaining the name of Christian. Norton and others of his ilk were anti-Christian not only because they were hypocritical, but also because they militated against "the distinct expression of ideas" which, Ripley said, "seem to me of vital importance to the welfare of man."[26]

The *Discourses* had been gleaned from sermons Ripley had delivered during the two years previous to publication ("Discourse V" having been published in *The Liberal Preacher* in November, 1835). The six essays are yoked neatly into pairs, and the first pair asserts that ideals exist and are of paramount importance when contrasted with material reality. The third discourse affirms that at least four ideals are inherent in man and constitute the Divine Image — the search for truth, the desire for Right to prevail, the instinct of fraternal love, the quest for self and social perfection. The fourth discourse insists that these four inherent elements need to be nurtured or else they will wither. The last pair of essays reiterate and intensify the themes of the previous four essays, climaxing with the promise from Matthew, "Blessed are the pure in heart, for they shall see God."

Within this general structure, Ripley had six main points to clarify — the fundamental nature of man, the power of intuitive reason to perceive godliness and to create beauty, the function and value of Christianity as a means for nurturing the soul, the practicality of Transcendentalism, the possibility that Transcendentalism might be wrong, and the tremendous promise that awaits those who believe. Ripley admits that, when ministers prate of the power of religion to make men partakers of the divine nature, "we at once think of the contrast which is presented by their actual condition." Exploitation of the worker, disregard of the poor, slavery, corruption, conceit, hypocrisy are everywhere present. To hear one preach the divinity of man and be aware of the human condition evokes "incredulity and almost despair." Evil, sin, and wrong certainly exist; but to look at only one side, the corrupt side of man, is narrow-minded and cycloptic. Such a pessimistic, one-eyed view does nothing to remedy the evil; it even encourages its spread.

Another side to man exists, a side at least as strong as the evil. Man can perceive truth; he can distinguish between right and wrong even if he seldom lives up to the truths he sees and the principles he believes. He is capable of disinterested love; and, though this virtue is rare, the perception of a state of perfection higher than man has ever reached is universal. Man's soul constantly "communes with an ideal perfectness which no human hand can ever call into being." These four aspirations, though they yet remain aspirations and not realizations, are sure proof of the imprint of God in man, they hint at man's destiny, and they prod him to attempt a closer approximation of the ideals he glimpses.

Man's basic nature is split, having a tremendous capacity for good and for evil. The four arguments of divinity will remain only seeds unless cultivated, and "This is accomplished . . . by calling forth native powers of the soul itself, not by forcing upon it any constraint or violence from without." Ripley here is of the Carlylean school that believes in saying "yea," in evoking the natural elements of divinity rather than in emphasizing the natural elements of evil through futile repression. Ripley's imagery in this passage from Discourse IV is organic: like plants, man's growth needs to be cultivated; the Puritans are wrong in stressing repression. To place man in a straitjacket only causes his demonic fury to grow and does nothing to bring forth the goodness within him. "Let our prisons be turned into hospitals," Ripley said; for care, not incarceration, is the proper corrective.

Having asserted the existence of man's divine nature, Ripley develops his view of intuitive reason — the faculty by which man recognizes the truths and the very existence of the soul. He once again confronts his old adversaries — the sensualist followers of Locke who maintain that all knowledge proceeds from a relationship with reality through the senses — by affirming that everyone intuits that some special essence lies within him. "Deny this idea who can — he cannot wholly deny his own Reason, — and though he may endeavor to cast it from him, it will return again, its voice will make itself heard, announcing the presence of the Almighty, and he cannot reject the conviction which it brings" (Discourse I). The five senses are valuable tools for acquiring knowledge, but intuitive reason is the one faculty that can give us knowledge of our super-sensual but natural divinity. "We think much of the evidence of sight — and justly, but the evidence of consciousness is more. We think we fully understand a subject which we have examined with our eyes, but there are some subjects which we understand the best from feeling them with our hearts" (Discourse IV). When man communes with Nature and when he communes with God, man is actually in communion with the better part of himself. This fact of communion which puts man in touch with eternal truths is inevitable and perennial; it is never to be denied completely or finally.

Although Ripley demotes sensualism to a secondary category, he does not mind using some of its analogies to argue for the portentous promise of Reason. He admits that the growth of the soul depends to a large degree on external influences, "but it is no less true that the outward universe is to a great degree dependent upon our souls for its character and influence, and that by changes in our inward condition, a corresponding change is produced in the objects with which we are surrounded" (Discourse II). Two men looking at the same scene from the same spot in a forest are capable of radically different responses. If one is depressed, he finds no beauty or joy in the sight. If the other's senses are heightened and his soul is alive, he enjoys an ecstasy of rapture in the scene. As it is with two men at the same place and time, so it is with a single man at different times or in different places: "It is from the cast and disposition of our souls that external nature derives its hues and conformations. . . . Forms are addressed to the eye, but the perception of beauty is in the soul" (Discourse II).

Ripley pushes this point to such an extreme that he virtually places God in the role of an artist who desperately needs an audience to verify the beauty of His creation. The eye receives colors, touch discovers textures, the ear records sounds; but these physical responses are meaningless unless the soul can create beauty out of the sense impressions it receives. "The sun might exist as the fountain of light . . . and pour forth its streams over the earth, but [without] the inward nature of man . . . the beauties of nature would be a lifeless blank, the variety of colors, of forms, of motions in the universe would be without significance, and the lavish bounty of Providence apparently bestowed in vain" (Discourse VI). If not for men, in short, God's efforts would be futile; and His presence, His truth, His beauty would be meaningless. God created a universe fraught with potential glory, but it remains lifeless until man discovers beauty — until man indeed re-creates beauty.

If Ripley seems to elevate man to a position equal to God's, this hint becomes a lucid assertion when he discusses Christianity. If he had shaken the Unitarian world in the Martineau review by stating that the human soul authenticates the Bible, he rattled Christendom in the *Discourses* by asserting that man authenticates God: "The human soul is the great argument for the Being and Perfection of God, and if we are insensible to this, we can have a living faith in no other." He warns the orthodox, "We look for the indications of his Being at too great a distance from ourselves instead of finding within our hearts such marks of his presence as would make him a felt and living reality" (Discourse VI). Since heart and soul are the essentials of existence, philosophies and theologies are useful for calling forth man's divine nature. Since Jesus was one man whose mind was so permeated with divine consciousness, whose whole nature was so truly in harmony with the divine purposes that he could say without presumption "that he and his Father were one," the followers of this man's example could feel sure that they were living correctly. Christianity or some other religion "of a spirit similar to that which [Christianity] contains" could be a successful incubator for the seeds of divinity within man.

But Christians who harp upon religion as a social code, as a special sect, or as a set of artificial rituals and petty regulations do much damage to the spirit. Christianity should be conceived of as

St. Peter did, "almost entirely in its practical bearings, as a system adopted to produce the most magnificent changes in the heart of man and the fortunes of the world" (Discourse III). In holding forth the promise of an afterlife, ministers have erred; for men have become so absorbed with obeying the letter of God's law in order to fulfill the requirements for admittance to heaven that they have neglected the spirit of religion and the possibilities of their own perfection. Ripley wants a religion that activates and electrifies the soul — not one that is obeyed with mechanical regularity, nor one that is so filled with vague reveries and mystical speculations that its members, "like the ancient philosopher who in gazing at the stars fell into a pit," would lose sight of its practical advantages.

But Ripley wants his own practical but not materialistic advantages. Making a statement that sounded most unAmerican to a nation intent on land speculation, industrial development, and expansion of its borders, Ripley said, "Man, with all his boasted improvements, has little control over the external universe. The world around us goes on, independent of our agency, without consulting our will. We cannot increase or diminish, to the amount of a single grain of sand, the quantity of matter of which the earth is composed. We cannot alter the time of the rising or the setting of a single star; . . . and all that man can do is to gaze in admiration or fall prostrate in reverence and joy" (Discourse II). Man is impotent when attempting to harness the universe; when succeeding in some little way, his materialistic mastery is trifling.

And rightly so, for this universe is not his province. His kingdom is within, and that is where he should concentrate his energies:

There he can exercise a rightful and commanding sway. Lord of himself, of the unseen powers of his own being, he can reign there with a more than kingly sovereignty. . . . The everlasting lights of the soul are called forth at his bidding, they are dimmed and sullied by his neglect, and upon his own will it depends whether they shine on in their radiant courses or fade in disastrous eclipse. Here is the consecrated sphere, in which his action may be effectual, which he may fill with brightness and purity and joy, or with darkness, pollution and despair. And is it not a greater privilege to be able to move the soul than it would be to reach the sun? . . . Is it not wise in us to give the strength of our souls to those things which are unseen and eternal, that we may thus consecrate those which are seen and temporal? (Discourse II)

Ripley holds forth the immense promise that man can become god-like, attain a state superior to Adam's, and create a state more glorious than Eden. He promises a rejuvenation — an elevation to a new and divine life whose nature man can not fully describe and whose pursuits he does not know.

But with the carrot comes the stick. Ripley knew he was appealing to the intuitive reason in each man's being, and he knew that this faculty could not be calibrated, mathematically defined, nor sensually perceived. The truths he uttered — truths he heard sounded by Pestalozzi in Switzerland, Coleridge in England, Schleiermacher in Germany, and Cousin in France — were truths whose acceptance hinged upon sympathetic responses from others' souls. Perhaps it all was folly, a grotesque mistake, or a fantastic dream? Yes, agreed Ripley; but, "if the Christian is guilty of folly in paying reverence to the unseen powers, give me his folly rather than the wisdom of one who by his own confession is a stranger to Reason, Conscience, to a sense of obligation, to the noblest faculties and attributes of man" (Discourse I).

All his life this point was the one about which Ripley was most passionate. He was sufficiently open-minded to recognize the possibility that he might be wrong in believing in man's divine nature, but he was not willing to give up hope because of this possibility. Perhaps God was an illusion, divinity a sham; perhaps chaos and meaninglessness were the order of the universe; but, since the matter could not be settled one way or the other to meet everyone's satisfaction through demonstrable proof, then Ripley would choose belief over doubt. "Do not deem him a man of a fantastic mind until you have proved that he is following phantoms" (Discourse I). At the very least, Ripley demonstrated his power of choice. Free to believe in nothingness and blankness or in divinity and a boundless future, he followed the direction in which his heart and soul led him.[27]

The *Discourses* obviously bear many similarities to Emerson's *Nature* which had been published two months earlier; both books emphasize the inner self, the transience and mutability of nature, the importance and greater reality of the ideal, the magnificent possibility of a Golden Age or a New Eden. But the *Discourses* are more direct, they are less poetic, and they lack the plethora of homely aphorisms found in *Nature.* However, the major difference between the two books is the matter of practicality. Both writers believed that man had a divine nature, but Emerson felt that man only needed to remove all the impediments, unclog the pipeline as it were, and divinity would flow forth. The two were never more in tune than at this time, for Ripley also said in Discourse IV, "Inspire [man's] soul with a filial love of God, and you make the world a paradise at once. Let all outward circumstances remain the same and correct the things that are unseen, you place his happiness on a secure foundation." But Ripley, the seeds of Brook Farm already germinating in his brain, also admitted that a great deal of nurturing is required to call forth divinity. However, he was not yet aware that the entire system of external forces would need to be revamped, a conviction that would capture him when he beheld the cruelty and ruthlessness of the Panic of 1837.

Emerson's *Nature* has become as famous as any piece of American literature while Ripley's *Discourses* are all but forgotten. In the contemporary scene, the situation was reversed. *Nature* had an impact upon budding Transcendentalists like Jones Very, Thoreau, and Ellery Channing; but, to existing Transcendentalists like Theodore Parker and Orestes Brownson who were to fight the good fight with powerful Unitarians and other American intellectuals, both documents were considered powerful summations of their collective aspirations and principles. In 1836, Convers Francis cited Ripley's *Discourses,* Bronson Alcott's *Questions on the Gospels,* and Brownson's *New Views* as the major pamphlets in the vanguard of the Transcendental movement; and Brownson himself acknowledged that he owed "more to [Ripley] than to any other man." When Alexander Kern says that Emerson did not emerge as a leader until after 1838 and when Sidney Ahlstrom asserts that Ripley was "the chief leader of the Transcendental movement during the central decade of its flowering time," they cannot be far from wrong. [28] Brownson, Theodore Parker, Charles Dana, John Sullivan Dwight, and James Freeman Clarke are but a few of those who looked to Ripley for leadership in this crucial time; and leadership he gave them.

V *The Crisis of 1839*

Ripley found himself the principal spokesman for those radical Unitarians who as yet lacked a unifying name. They were called proponents of the "New Views" by Orestes Brownson, the "Believers" by Ripley, and "the Spiritualists" by Convers Francis.

One of their most formidable opponents — Francis Bowen — supplied these rebels with a comprehensive label. Providing a balanced view of the two Unitarian factions, James Walker complemented Ripley's preface and translation of Ullman's aphorisms in the *Christian Examiner* for January, 1837, with Francis Bowen's review of Emerson's *Nature.*[29] Bowen, who disliked "the vein of mysticism" in *Nature,* used Emerson's pamphlet as an excuse to attack all those Unitarians whom he branded "Transcendentalists," giving them the name by which they would be known to the world forever.

Bowen's essay, as Cameron Thompson insists, must be considered as part of the continuing Norton-Ripley controversy. Curiously, no direct reply was made by any of the Transcendentalists, perhaps because Bowen, unlike Norton, tried to understand Transcendentalism, even sympathized with some of its arguments, and offered criticism which seemed constructive, at least to Ripley. When Bowen said that "the observation of sensible phenomena can lead only to the discovery of insulated, partial and relative laws; but the same consideration of the same phenomena, in a typical point of view, may lead us to infinite and absolute truth — to a knowledge of the reality of things," he grasped the core of Emerson's and Ripley's philosophy. Unlike Norton, Bowen was not reacting emotionally from blind prejudice.

When he turned one of Ripley's basic critiques of Unitarianism against him by claiming that the Transcendentalists in their lofty, imaginative flights threatened to set themselves apart from the common man, Ripley was forced to stop and take stock. When Bowen had said that Transcendentalism "rejects the aid of observation and will not trust to experiment," he had implied that no practical effort had been made to create an environment in which the supposed four elements of inherent divinity could flower. Ripley felt that Bowen's criticism, if not valid, required at least a concrete rebuttal. In the summer of 1838, he took a trip to the West because he needed some time alone to reassess his views as a Transcendentalist and to conceive of an experiment that would rebut Bowen's charge. He emerged from the 1838 trip with the Brook Farm idea burning in his brain and was transformed from a Transcendental intellectual without a definite program in mind to a militant Transcendentalist.

From 1836 to 1838, however, Ripley's main task was to lead the new school of thought. He needed to discover who the Transcendentalists were, what they stood for, and what they could do. To accomplish this task, he organized three plans of attack: seek out Thomas Carlyle who seemed the sole living Englishman who believed in Transcendentalism, organize regular meetings of the group which would later become known as the Transcendental Club, and head a mammoth editorial project called *Specimens of Foreign Standard Literature,* fourteen volumes of translations which would demonstrate to Americans the widespread breadth and respectability of Transcendental thoughts abroad.

Carlyle's Novemer, 1834, letter to Emerson was so marked by depression that Ripley composed an effulgent reply which he was reluctant to send. At Emerson's urging, he did mail a revised version on June 1, 1835, that still contained such precious lines as, "I am impelled by a yearning sympathy to raise my voice to your ear across the wide waste of waters over which the music of your soul-melody has sounded to this distant spot."[30] Receiving no reply and fearing that his streak of "good little boy-ness" had misrepresented him once again, Ripley sent a second letter on December 29, 1836, explaining that, if the first letter had seemed too extravagant or too enthusiastic, it was only because "of the earnestness with which a true voice is welcomed here . . . the greater as such voices are seldom heard among us — the din of business and politics well nigh drowning all sounds from the heavenly mount."[31]

In this letter, Ripley mentioned his 1836 battle with Andrews Norton whose "prodigious sarcasm and almost infallible accuracy" spread terror wherever he spoke; he also enclosed his latest writings which he had hoped would aid somewhat to crack the "thick crust of blind conservatism" in Boston, "one of the most aristocratic cities in the world." Suffering under Norton's abuse and leading a movement that was but dimly defined, Ripley earnestly called upon Carlyle for mutual support, hailing him "as a brother in this . . . holy hope," but Carlyle's response was silence. He never answered Ripley's plea and even belittled his later Brook Farm effort in the last chapter of *Past and Present* when he denigrated the group of "Socinian ministers" who sought to reform the world by cultivating onions.

In spite of this rebuff, Ripley continued to admire Carlyle and praised his anti-capitalist stands in *The Harbinger* for June, 1845.

He admired the hero in Carlyle's *Life of John Sterling* (1851) as a virile man of earnest and reflective temperament who possessed great insights because he valued freedom of thought, loved mankind, and hated bigotry and sham — an heroic model that Ripley hoped he himself fulfilled.[32] But, by 1858, Ripley had so outgrown Carlyle that he assailed "the worship of mere force of will and strong animal impulse" in *Heroes and Hero Worship* and in *Past and Present.* By 1876, Ripley, though he respected Carlyle as an intellectual pioneer, ranked him as a "has-been."[33]

Receiving no support from Carlyle in these formative years from 1836 to 1840, Ripley concentrated on his native scene to see what could be done to crystallize the Transcendental movement. On September 8, 1836, at F. H. Hedge's suggestion, Ripley met with George Putnam and Emerson at Willard's Hotel in Cambridge to form a "symposium" to discuss the moods of the times. From that autumn afternoon stroll grew the Transcendental Club whose first meeting was held at Ripley's Boston house on September 19, 1836, with Alcott, Channing, J. F. Clarke, James Walker, and others in attendance.[34]

The Club met some thirty times in the next four years, and its only rule was never to invoke the exclusive principle so that freedom of speech would prevail. Ripley attended almost all the meetings, influenced the selection of topics, and participated so effectively in discussion that he moved Theodore Parker to describe an exchange between Channing and him as the equal of one of Plato's dialogues.[35] As long as the discussion remained speculative, the group enjoyed harmony; but, when some members spoke of practical measures, as when a journal to put their decisive views into print was proposed at the September 18, 1839, mccting, many of the members balked.

By this time, Ripley had grown more militant and felt that the Club had outgrown its usefulness. When Parker and Clarke tried to revive the Club in the 1850's, Ripley was not interested. The Club had performed its duty and was no longer needed. It had given the avant-garde thinkers an opportunity to gather to see exactly who were the members of the new school and to gain a sense of unity on general principles if not on specific issues. Most of all, the Transcendental Club gave its members the chance to thrash out their ideas and to achieve clarity as to what precisely their beliefs were. By doing so, they assured themselves that they were not operating in a vacuum but were charting the intellectual course of the future.

With utmost confidence, then, the Transcendentalists met the Crisis of 1839 which Norton brought to a head. When Norton bitterly indicted Transcendentalism as "The Latest Form of Infidelity" in his speech before the Cambridge Divinity School on July 19, 1839, he was reacting to three major aggravations. First, Emerson's Divinity School Address of July, 1838, had scorned the school of biblical scholarship (of which Norton was a principal) as a cold, lifeless, meaningless method. Second, in the *Boston Quarterly Review* of January, 1839, Brownson blithely had dismissed Norton's life's work, *The Evidence of the Genuineness of the Four Gospels* (1838) as irrelevant and as antithetical to modern America. Third, Ripley had published the first two volumes of *Specimens of Foreign Standard Literature* which, while repeating much of the material in the *Christian Examiner* articles, differed from them because it broadcasted his Transcendental heresies to all literate Americans instead of tamely offering his views to fellow ministers for their private consideration.

Feeling backed against the wall, Norton lashed out savagely at the Transcendentalists, ridiculed their ideas, accused them of scholarly incompetence, called them infidels, and cited two of Ripley's favorite philosophers — Spinoza and Schleiermacher — as the principal European heretics. When Norton left the protection of a collegiate address and entered the public arena by publishing his speech as an independent pamphlet, everybody, as Perry Miller says, looked to Ripley as the Transcendentalists' spokesman to reply.[36]

Relishing this opportunity to revenge Norton's surprise attack of 1836, but also regretting having to take time to finish this battle when more important matters had to be attended to, Ripley replied in three lengthy essays in 1839 and 1840 called "The Latest Form of Infidelity Examined: A First, Second and Third Letter Addressed to Mr. Andrews Norton." Ripley's basic complaints were that Norton's logic was loose, his manner rude, his tone dictatorial, and his ideas outdated. Even though Ripley overreacted to Norton's charge of scholarly incompetence with nearly five hundred pages of tedious scholarly references, his answer was considered superb by his fellow Transcendentalists. Theodore Parker called it "excellent, both in design and execution."[37]

Significantly, when Parker framed his own reply, using as

spokesman a plain-speaking Westerner called Levi Blodgett (1840), he substituted for Ripley's four divine elements "the existence of God and man's sense of dependence upon him as given in man's nature."[38] In spite of Ripley's leadership and in spite of the crystallizing effect of the Club meetings, the Transcendentalists still held highly personal and diverse views. Ripley and Parker, supposedly presenting a united front, nevertheless differed greatly on orthodoxy.

Ripley himself was wading in a divided stream as the letters to Norton show. On one hand, he claimed that Norton was a papist because he separated the minister from his flock by insisting that truth be "drawn from grammars and lexicons and mouldy traditions, not from the treasures of the human heart."[39] Ultimately, according to Norton, only scholars can be Christians, a concept Ripley believed abhorrent to Christianity. At the same time, in insisting on the truth of the human heart, Ripley ran the risk of separating everyone from everyone else. If each man should trust primarily to the beckonings of his intuition, was there not the danger of no man's heeding his neighbor?

While Emerson could accept this possibility as a necessary situation and while both Emerson and Ripley believed that the human heart was everywhere similar when reduced to fundamentals, Ripley felt the need for a check-and-balance system to test the truths each individual intuits: "True learning, in my opinion, is as modest as it is inquisitive; it searches for truth with a lowly and reverent aspect; it never counts itself to have attained; it never presumes to assert that it can gain no further light on any subject; conscious of frailty, it communes with all wise teachers; and in meek self-dependence, compares the lessons they announce with the oracles of God."[40] Emerson's heroic self-reliance becomes "meek self-dependence" in Ripley. The human heart remains the primary, initial, and ultimate source of truth; but Ripley emphasizes the importance of referring, though not deferring, to the recorded insights of others.

If Norton's bigotry provoked Ripley to radical thought, Francis Bowen's reasoned criticism prevented him, for better or worse, from pushing to extremes. More than ever, Ripley felt the need for a community of seekers, a group of thoughtful souls who, by searching the inmost recesses of their hearts, might authenticate the divine principles Ripley cited in his *Discourses, Examiner* articles, and speeches. More than ever, Ripley required an experiment that would test the spirit, but he first had to fulfill his obligations as Transcendental chieftain.

VI Specimens of Literature

Ripley's career as a clergyman can be divided into three distinct phases. From his Harvard graduation in 1823 until 1836, he sought to perfect the sect of which he was a minister. From the date of Norton's public attack on November 5, 1836, until the galley proofs of *Specimens of Foreign Standard Literature* were ready in mid-1838, Ripley was a Transcendental intellectual. His own ideas and principles were clear to him, but the group which he led was vague about underlying principles and was confused over practical objectives. The movement grew out of Unitarianism, but powerful Unitarians assailed it as heretical. Some of its main impetus came from Thomas Carlyle, but he declined contact with any member but Emerson. Its very name was given not by one of its own members but by one of its most effective critics. From 1838 until Brook Farm became a Socialist experiment in 1845, Ripley had a clear idea of the kind of Transcendentalism he represented. He turned militant and sought to realize his creed as a living faith among as many of his countrymen as possible.

The *Specimens of Foreign Standard Literature* is a clear transition between these last two phases. It was published in fourteen volumes from 1838 to 1842 under Ripley's editorship with the various Transcendentalists contributing an introduction and translations of their favorite foreign writers, philosophers, theologians, and historians. Ripley wrote the first two volumes on Victor Cousin, Theodore Jouffroy, and Benjamin Constant which were titled *Philosophical Miscellanies;* and his purpose was spelled out in the introduction to the first volume. No longer should the Transcendental intellectual stand apart from society and converse only with fellow intelligentsia and defend his faith from the attacks of clergymen. Rather,

> The office of the true scholar in our republic is to connect himself in the most intimate and congenial relations with the energetic and busy population of which he is too often merely an insignificant unit. He is never to stand aloof from the concerns of the people; . . . he is never to set himself above them as their condescending instructor; . . . but he is called upon to

honor the common mind, to commune with the instinctive experiences of the mighty heart of a free nation, and to bring the aid of learning and philosophy to the endeavor of the people to comprehend their destiny and to secure its accomplishment. [41]

The intention of the *Specimens* was to assist the American populace in achieving its destiny by showing how its impulses were consonant with philosophical advances. In a letter to Convers Francis in 1837, Ripley stated that, with the completion of the *Specimens,* ". . . we should have a library which would do honor to our land and enlarge the cultivation of our people." [42] During his lifetime Ripley was to undertake three mammoth editorial projects — *Specimens* (1838), *Handbook on Literature and the Fine Arts* (1852), and *The American Encyclopedia* (1862) — each of which had the general intention of education and elevation with each successive cyclopedia getting nearer to the level of the average American.

This goal, of course, was factitious. Ripley wanted to give the people what he felt they needed, not what they said they wanted; only through a nimble mental gymnastic could he equate want with need. Harvard-bred Ripley was still élitist in attempting to convince his countrymen that they could understand better the promptings of their hearts if they were familiar with Constant, Jouffroy, and Cousin. The *Specimens,* for all its claims as a militant document, remained a product of the speculative period of Transcendentalism.

This dichotomy dogged all the Transcendentalists. Like Whitman and Thoreau, Ripley was torn between democratic principles and selective heroism. The chief paradox of Transcendentalism is its glorifying human potentiality while complaining of actual human performance. Superficially addressed to the masses, the *Specimens'* main audience was fellow intellectuals. Ripley even asked Henry Wadsworth Longfellow to contribute "1 or 2 German poems or songs" so that his signature would lend respectability to the project. [43] This ploy was meant to convince social pillars that to be familiar with Continental literature was not necessarily to be morally lax.

Besides attempting to overcome widespread prejudice against foreign culture, Ripley sought to win his countrymen's acceptance by proving the universality of the Transcendental movement. The emphasis was on the word "Standard," stressing the point that these were not radical European notions but harbingers of the new movement with which America must hasten to keep step. As the

Miltonic epigraph stipulated, ". . . so must ripe understanding . . . be imported into our minds from foreign writings [or we shall] come short in the attempts of any great enterprise." Ripley's main appeal was to the Puritanical belief that history is the gradual unfolding of God's will on earth. The *Specimens* would prove that "A spirit is abroad, free, bold, uncompromising, and terrible as an army with banners, which is trying the opinions and institutions of the world as by fire." The duty of the wise and the good is to be aware of these advances in order to promote progress.

In 1942, René Welleck said that the effect of German philosophy on American Transcendentalism has "never been studied in any detail." Today, the subject has been thoroughly investigated: but the investigators have often lost Welleck's balanced perspective that the relationship between the two cultures was one of contact as opposed to influence.[44] Brownson had said in 1837 that "Germany reaches us only through France," and the fact that eleven of the fourteen volumes of the *Specimens* are devoted to German writers means merely that the Transcendentalists wished to study the sources of the ideas which Madame DeStaël, Carlyle, and Coleridge had popularized.

Ripley himself had serious reservations about the Germans. In a *Harbinger* article (VI, 1848), he said that German philosophy tries to "explain the universe or the human soul by the mere force of thought without the scientific analysis of facts" which is "as absurd as the attempt to leap over one's head." His own preference was for the French method, especially Victor Cousin's "Eclecticism" which Norton asailed as too vague and which Emerson thought not vague enough. Ripley's most succinct definition was that Eclecticism was ". . . not an arbitrary picking and choosing here and there of notions that seemed fitted to be wrought into a sort of metaphysical mosaic, but a scientific procedure founded, in reality, on the necessary laws of human thought." Sensualism, Idealism, Skepticism, Mysticism are partial systems which are erroneous when they exclude other systems; for "Each contains a portion of truth, reflects a certain aspect of reality, has its prototype in the essential laws of the universe. A perfect philosophy must combine the elements of truth involved in each system."[45]

Ripley here is backing away from the extreme to which Norton had pushed him. In giving an intellectual history of the eighteenth century, Ripley claims that Sir Francis Bacon's stress on externals had been extended by Hobbes to mean that the evidence of the senses is the only reliable information; and Ripley reveres Locke for directing attention back to the workings of the mind. Not able to cast aside his training as a scholar, he modifies his statements in the *Discourses* and seeks to reconcile the promptings of the Transcendental soul with scientific investigation. Cousin is thereby respected for the orderly arrangement of his arguments and for his rigorous reasoning which serve to verify psychological needs.

Ripley's main goal is to achieve "the wedded union of philosophy and faith," to bring intellectual interests and psychological needs into alignment.[46] To do so, he streamlines the four divine elements of the *Discourses* to focus on one — man's destiny.

> The phenomenon of [pure] reason, conceiving the idea of destiny, conceiving that every being has its destiny, and that this destiny sustains a necessary relation to that of the Universe, is not produced in the mind of man during the first period of his existence on earth. The day that it is produced is a memorable one in his history, one that he can never forget; but it is one that delays its arrival, and until it arrives we may say that the existence of man is only the highest degree of animal existence. (*Specimens,* I, 286)

Unless man can conceive of a state of perfection far superior to his present life, he remains no more than a sophisticated brute.

According to Ripley, many conceptions of destiny are artificial or erroneous; but the fact that so many have held to a belief in destiny, despite failures and delusions, testifies to the presence of pure reason. Were man indeed living in the best of all possible worlds, he would be enjoying as much harmony as possible; and reason would never wake to prick man for his imperfection. Hence evil is a necessary element. Suffering surprises man as much as it appalls him, indicating that man wishes the universe to be set right. Hunger, misery, and frustration cause bitterness; and bitterness is valuable for it makes man ask why he is here and why the world is out of tune. Man can learn to adapt to an imperfect world, but his initial and fundamental reaction to imperfection is shock and a desire for correction. This sense of destiny, intuited by reason which is awakened by evil, is the chief quality that raises man above the animals. The job of man, his necessary obligation if he intends to fulfill his potential, is to strive to realize his destiny regardless of manifold failures and frustrations.

Jouffroy, Cousin, and Constant approached the matter of destiny from different angles. Of the three, Constant is the most vigorous; he agrees with Ripley that evil is "This deep sense of want [which] is intimately connected with the religious sentiment." This iconoclastic, non-sectarian, French revolutionary knew that "revolutions are not for the sake of dethroning kings, but of exalting men; not to strip off the glories of the past, but to throw a new glory around the future. . ." (II, 276, 264). Jouffroy emphasizes "the collective wisdom of the race," a transcendence of individuality which William James praises in *The Varieties of Religious Experience* and which parallels Ripley's belief that an individual's perception of truth must be tested by the perceptions of other thinkers. All three — Jouffroy, Cousin, and Constant — stress the importance of developing all one's faculties, the intellect as well as intuition, and the necessity of approaching every philosophical system with a mind open to the best parts of every philosophy.

Cousin praised Ripley's project as a milestone in promoting sound intellectual methodology.[47] The *Specimens* raised the hackles of the old guard and allowed more liberal thinkers to peruse the primary source materials about which they had heard so much. But the volumes did little to promote the ferment of social reform. Militant in objective but informative in effect, the *Specimens'* main usefulness was to give the Transcendentalists a project to rally around, thereby affording them time and opportunity to crystallize their thoughts under the guise of taking positive action.

VII The Dial

The *Specimens* were born of Ripley's first confrontation with Norton in 1836. Having translated the views of foreign Transcendentalists, it was time for Americans to publish their own. When the Norton-Ripley controversy escalated in 1839, the birth of *The Dial,* the most famous Transcendental group project, was almost inevitable. Since almost all journals were now closed to the Transcendentalists and since the Norton-Ripley controversy raged so fiercely, Ripley lobbied hard for a Transcendental organ. On September 18, 1839, the die was cast in spite of strong resistance from Hedge and other club members. Bronson Alcott suggested the name; Margaret Fuller accepted the editorship; and Ripley, because of his practical success with the *Specimens,* agreed to handle "all the business part." *The Dial* — "a gallant effort to conduct a free and critical and literate journal," as Perry Miller phrases it — was born.

From the outset Ripley's responsibilities entailed much more than distribution, subscription, printing, and finance. James F. Clarke, upset by the radical nature of a piece on Schleiermacher, urged Ripley to omit it from the second number of *The Dial.* Ripley's response to his close friend was as vigorous as the article: ". . . we must be governed by a sense of integrity towards the author, rather than of compassion towards the reader. Besides a few tough passages of the kind you allude to are of good use to aid the digestion of the rest, just as chickens thrive better with a little gravel to their corn."[48] Ripley's role as editor in defending freedom of thought and forceful expression was second only to Fuller's in the first two years of *The Dial.*

Ripley added to the aggressive tone of the periodical with his own essays. In his analysis of "Brownson's Writings" in the *Dial* of July, 1840 (22-46), he praised three main points: all things are holy, the Godhead must be sought in the soul of man, and the dream of a New Eden was feasible. In "A Letter to a Theological Student" in October, 1840 (183-87), he pursued his attack on "liberal" ministers by claiming that they were as repressive as orthodox ones and that theology, when compared to other disciplines, was "a decrepit, worn and withered figure." He furthermore reiterated the two values for which he had become famous — tolerance and open-mindedness as necessary criteria for intellectual honesty. In a third article, "The Art of Life, the Scholar's Calling," he struck a new note by insisting that the crucial need of the times was for a reformer whose intentions were honorable and whose efforts were practical.[49] "What the age requires is not books but example, high, heroic example; not words but deeds; not societies but men, — men who shall have their root in themselves and attract and convert the world. . . ." Ironically, this article implies that *The Dial* and the club which fostered it are superficial in terms of social impact — a suspicion that would soon become Ripley's conviction.

All the Transcendentalists berated *The Dial,* and Ripley himself was disappointed. He lamented that "They had expected hoofs and horns while it proved as gentle as any sucking dove."[50] But he was more pleased with *The Dial* than most, for it did rattle those who "bow down to the huge shapeless idols of brass and clay." He was delighted to inform John S. Dwight that *The Dial* had shaken both political parties. Democrats and Whigs alike scurried to broadcast that they had no connection with nor sympathy for the new Transcendental enterprise. The periodical ". . . has produced a decided sensation. I feared it would fall dead, but there is no dread of that now. People seem to look on with wonder, while the Philistines who dare show themselves are wrathy as fighting cocks." As a means of waking his neighbors from their complacency, Ripley was happy that *The Dial* was somewhat successful.

But the periodical was meant to meet another objective, and its success on this score was by no means certain. Ripley spoke hopefully that ". . . the *Dial* will not only show how high the sun is up, but reflect a welcome, a healing light over our dark places." It was one thing to make his neighbors' eyes grow wide with wonder, but it was quite another to make them see truth. To accomplish the latter, *The Dial* did not suffice; a more dramatic example was necessary. In October, 1840, he told Emerson that his *Dial* pieces which expressed the Transcendentalists' thoughts so clearly caused him feelings of "true joy," but they also made him feel more and more restless to have some of those ideals put into practice. He could not be "happy without the attempt to realize them." [51]

Ripley was now convinced that only an experiment like Brook Farm could show the world that Transcendentalists could practice what they preached. He promised Emerson, "I hope you will yet see some of your visions made substantial in the 'city of God' which we shall try to build." *The Dial* lasted a mere four years, never made any money, and attracted no more than three hundred subscribers. The journal had hooves to kick, but it could not pull the vehicle of human progress forward. *The Dial* was meant to show how high the sun of the New Age was up, and Ripley feared it indicated that the sun had not yet cleared the horizon. He hoped that Brook Farm would be a more accurate and favorable sun-dial, perhaps even a sun itself to light the way to the New Age.

VIII *Loomings*

Ripley spent the last two years of his ministry preparing for his Brook Farm experiment. The salient milestone that marked this more militant phase was his trip to the West in 1838. He had been looking forward to the trip since 1837 when James Freeman Clarke's letters from Cincinnati made the West seem vigorous and the East effete. In March, 1837, Ripley complained that Boston was full of "filtered Conservatives and Conventionalists" who were masquerading as liberals. The East overflowed with "painted and hollow shows" while the West seemed vibrant and alive.[52]

He finally got to see the West in the summer of 1838. Since completing the manuscripts for the *Specimens* had caused so much damage to his eyes that he feared he might go entirely blind, the Western trip was a time for recuperation and reflection as well as an opportunity for novel experiences. As he traveled as far west as Chicago and as far north as Lake Superior, he led a wandering and casual life, going for weeks without reading an Eastern newspaper, encountering "no more Transcendental problems . . . than the best mode of crossing the State of Michigan."[53] While in Cleveland, Ohio, he heard that Emerson had rocked the Unitarian world with his Divinity School Address, but Cambridge seemed a world away and the splash Emerson had made caused the merest ripple in Ohio.

Ohioans nevertheless proved themselves "good Americans." "Society, wherever I have been, is the incarnation of the actual; everything is postponed to business, and business is to make bargains and thus to make money." But, in spite of their materialism, the Westerners cheered Ripley with their genuine enthusiasm for the New Views. This was a sure sign that Norton's conservatism was waning, that Transcendental ideas were to be the movement of the future, and that Transcendentalism was not an isolated New England phenomenon. To Ripley, "Of illiberal liberal Christianity I find not one. Our Cambridge Conservatism can do nothing here; but young men with the glow of life in their souls and the word of power on their lips need no better sphere than these noble citadels of traffic present. I see nothing which is to save the West from the . . . worship of Mammon but setting forth the great principles of human nature" which the Transcendentalists preached.

Ripley grew convinced that the present obsession with business and money was but a "transition life," a prelude to the New Age. "It is temporary," he told Dwight, "and we may both live long enough to look back with incredulous wonder on this period of our land's history." The West reinforced Ripley's faith in the possibility of man and America. The frontier inspired him so that he felt "more than half-disposed to turn Missionary 'for good,' and leave my books to moulder. . . ." The brilliant Harvard scholar had had his second commencement. He was now prepared to fight for those principles he believed essential; his resolve was firm; the opportunity would soon come.

He returned to Boston a more forceful proponent of militant Transcendentalism who would settle for no less than dissociation from all conventional institutions, including his own church, but not until he delivered a few broadsides against the hypocrisy and the materialism of the times. Since he had been called an infidel, he preferred a full disclosure of his heresies. He was "a peace man, a temperance man, an abolitionist, a transcendentalist, a friend of radical reform in our social institutions," and he accepted any other labels that opposed inhumane conventions and smug complacency. He still considered himself a Christian in that he had to "aid in the overthrow of every form of slavery; I would free the mind from bondage and the body from chains."[54]

In "The Claims of the Age on the Work of the Evangelist," which he delivered at the ordination of John Sullivan Dwight, Ripley advised that, if a man insisted on remaining a priest, he should strive to create an ideal Christian community consisting of "a band of brothers emancipated by submission to Christ from all external authority." This work was a noble one, but it was unfortunately limited to parish precincts. How much nobler to work actively as a reformer to make God's will manifest on earth. How much more effective to create "the prevalence of righteousness in human institutions" where war, violence, greed, and slavery were abolished. Achieving a personal experience of God was laudable, but the hope of the world was the establishment of the "spirit of Christ in the institutions of men; on this depends the redemption of humanity."[55] In the *Discourses on the Philosophy of Religion,* Ripley had insisted that "the Kingdom of God is within"; he now added that the duty of a Christian was to strive to create a kingdom of God without, that "the work of the Evangelist . . . would shake and agitate society" so that justice would prevail over selfishness and the rule of love over force.

In demanding maximum freedom from authority, Ripley ran the risk of advocating irresponsible license. The built-in governor, of course, was Christian principles. But what if one's intuitive perception of these principles were in error? What if one's supposed vision of God were really inspired by Satan? Ripley thought this development highly improbable. But, if the error did occur, correction could be supplied through "Common Sense."[56] In the *Specimens,* he had spoken of the need to verify one's intuitive glimpses by referring to the insights of other "serious and devoted thinkers." Now he carried the idea one step further and used common sense to stand for the "popular mind." Ideals would be tested in the fire of human experience. Personal insight could be verified by the response it received from a community of sympathetic and sincere souls. The popular mind could be trusted, Ripley believed, for it had established cults around Christ and Buddha but not around Genghis Khan nor Attila the Hun.

The importance of community in encouraging and verifying personal insight made a communal experiment appear more and more necessary to Ripley. A Thoreauvian cabin or an Emersonian study could not satisfy his desire to agitate and shake society; moreover, either one might cultivate eccentricity instead of divinity. Community was, therefore, an essential safeguard against idiosyncrasy. The idea had germinated. When he vacationed at Theodore Parker's farm at West Roxbury a few miles outside Boston in the summer of 1840, he found the place.

If Ripley were going to test the practicality of the New Views, he wanted the investigation of Transcendental theories to continue. He had to make sure that in his absence the less militant Transcendentalists had an established program for assessing their principles. Consequently, he arranged for Margaret Fuller's "Conversation Classes" to be held at his home in Boston. These sessions ran from March 1, 1841, to 1844; and they focused on two questions; "What were we born to do?" and "How shall we do it?" According to Caroline Healy Dall, the main impetus for the Conversation Classes sprang from the interest in Brook Farm and accounted for the distinguished attendance.[57] Ripley seemed to Dall "to be more conscious of the movement of the world than any of our party." He proved an aggressive and valuable member and was responsible to a large extent for the success of the first four meetings. Leaving his less militant Transcendental friends in Fuller's capable hands, Ripley was now prepared to take the Brook Farm plunge.

CHAPTER 3

Brook Farm: Transcendental Trial

I *Reasons*

HOW does one become a hero? Ripley had tried to promote heroism in his Purchase Street congregation, but his listeners had not responded to the call, probably, Ripley surmised, because the social structure prevented them. He had attempted to transform the Unitarian Society into a church of all saints, but powerful ministers had vehemently balked his efforts. Since Ripley wanted to accomplish something positive, not merely to debate, he left the church hoping that time and the pugnacious Theodore Parker would work the transformation. Like Parker, Ripley gave his help to various reform movements from antislavery to labor reform; but, like Emerson, he had little faith that these isolated, piecemeal reforms would bring about the revolution of human nature that the Transcendentalists demanded. He had helped found the Transcendental Club, but he was impatient with its inaction. If the members were so reticent about establishing *The Dial,* what timid leaders they would make in regenerating society.

Nevertheless, Ripley broached the subject to the Transcendental coterie in the fall of 1840,[1] explaining the general plans for his community. He exhorted that the Transcendentalists had a chance to put into practice what they preached and to build the city of God to which they gave lip service. The results were as might be expected: the Club recoiled from this ambitious endeavor. Thus resulted one of the keenest paradoxes in the history of Transcendentalism. Of the original founders of Brook Farm, the most serious social test of Transcendental principles, only one claimed to be a Transcendentalist. Other Transcendentalists, like Charles A. Dana and John Sullivan Dwight, would join the commune later; others, like Emerson and Margaret Fuller, would be frequent visitors; but George Ripley was the sole Transcendentalist willing to

Florida. Following the Pilgrim example, most of the later communities sought to establish alternatives to the prevailing socioeconomic-religious system. Fifty-three communes had been sown from 1694 to 1840, and more than two-thirds that number were founded in the four-year period from 1840 to 1844. Reacting to the Panic of 1837, to the spirit of Romanticism, and to the American tradition of protest by community, communes sprang up from A to Z — from the Amana colony in Iowa to the Zoarites in Ohio. Some fancied free-love principles; some detested private property; some were religious fanatics; but many saw their efforts not as an escape from society but as a way to register dissatisfaction and to show America how she might improve. To this last type of commune Brook Farm belongs. As Ripley explained to Emerson, he could asily make Brook Farm into a pastoral retreat from society or into personal idyll, but Ripley's bent was toward ideals, not idylls: "Personally, my tastes and habits would lead me in another direc- on. I have a passion for being independent of the world, and of ery man in it. This I could do easily on the estate; . . . But I feel und to sacrifice this private feeling in the hope of a great social od. . . ."[4] Ripley had every confidence that self-culture, the de- lopment of god-like potentiality in the individual, was possible ly if persons were so assured of a steady income that they could ford time to spend on self-culture.

Ripley believed that Transcendentalism was the wave of the ture. One day the Golden Age would dawn when all would knowledge the wisdom of seeking self-culture. Perhaps that day ad arrived. Margaret Fuller declined to join the commune, saying "We are not ripe to reconstruct society." But how do we know without a trial? Ripley argued. Brook Farm would test society to see if it were ready for Transcendentalism. Using a metaphor that Thoreau would later echo to conclude *Walden,* Ripley told Emerson in a letter of November 9, 1840, that Brook Farm, "if wisely executed, will be a light over this country and age. If not the sunrise, it will be the morning star."

He hoped Emerson would join because Emerson's decision would "do much towards settling the question with me, whether the time has come for the fulfillment of a high hope, or whether the work belongs to a future generation." Emerson declined since he believed with Fuller that Society was not yet ready for an awakening, and because he feared losing his individuality in a commune.

make this bold move. Of the financial backing, one-th
from proclaimed Transcendentalists; the rest, from other
If Ripley had been surprised to find he had shocked
Unitarians with his Transcendental radicalism, he was bemu
discover that he had also frightened his fellow Transcendentali

The motivation behind this dramatic venture involves ha
dozen factors. On one hand, festered contempt for capitalism;
the other, blistered fear of bloody revolution. In 1840, t
disastrous Panic of 1837 had four years yet to run. The economi
machinery had exposed its flaws and had mercilessly ground the
worker and the poor in its gears with only irresponsibility or
hypocrisy on the part of politicians and capitalists. Even when
running smoothly, the system reeked odiously, for its lubricants
were greed and rapacious competitiveness. Because of these
motivations and circumstances, the Transcendentalists feared a
violent reaction. Parker warned that, "if powerful men will not
write justice with black ink on white paper, ignorant and violent
men will write it on the soil in letters of blood. . . ." Brownson in
1840 vociferated that the rich business community would neve
consent to the demands of the masses, for such demands can "b
effected only by the strong arm of physical force" resulting in
"war the like of which the world as yet has never witnessed."
Ripley's community was to be the golden mean between th
destructiveness of capitalism and the debacle of war. He hoped tha
Brook Farm could either supplant capitalism without destroyin
the people who ran it or co-exist with it.

Two other reasons arise from the spirit of the age; the passion fo
reforms of all kinds and for communes in particular. Emerson tol
Carlyle in 1840 that "We are all a little wild here with numberle
projects of social reform," and the Chardon Street Convention
November verified his sentiments. Many gathered, the young a
the old, the zealous and the confused, "madmen, madwomen, m
with beards, Dunkers, Muggletonians, Come-outers, Groar
Agrarians . . . Abolitionists, Calvinists, Unitarians," w
commonality was that they "were in search of something bette
more satisfying than a vote or a definition."[3] Their concern w
less than the possibility and practical means of universal re
but, of the entire melange of social movers, none was mo
pressive than the communards. America had been founded
bands of closely knit comrades in Massachusetts, Virgin

He further objected that the Brook Farm plan was too comfortable and not ascetic and Spartan-like. But he praised Ripley's heroism and prayed that Ripley's estimation of the readiness of America to awaken was correct. Undeterred at being the only Transcendentalist to have enough faith in his project to make it a reality, Ripley carried through his intention to dip his Transcendental toe in the mainstream of American life to see if the temperature were right.

Even if the Brazen Age were not ripe for transformation into a Golden Age, the Brook Farm experiment could be highly useful as propaganda for Transcendentalism. As early as 1827, Ripley wrote in his journal that, if philosophers wanted to do more than merely exchange views over tea-cups, if they desired to affect the general populace and influence the entire fabric of society, they needed a forceful and dramatic vehicle to present their ideas:

> One cause of the *apparent* success of fanatical over rational Christianity may be found in the definite object at which the fanatic aims; he strives to produce a given effect upon the mind which may be stated in so many words; he places before us the point to which he exhorts us to arrive. The rational Christian on the other hand must needs be more general; he strives to produce the gradual but universal improvement of the character, and of course he has nothing so direct to present to man's attention. Just as it is easy to excite a populace to enthusiasm in favor of a man or party; but hard to make them good patriots.[5]

Since the pulpit had been ineffective in spreading Transcendentalism and since *The Dial,* like the *Specimens* and *Discourses,* would probably also reach only the intelligentsia, Brook Farm would serve as a vivid example of living Transcendentalism to the entire social body of America.

As Caroline H. Dall, one historian of Transcendentalism, has remarked, ". . . we owe the most permanent results of the Transcendental movement to the enthusiasm kindled and sustained at Brook Farm." Even such a tough-minded anti-Transcendentalist as Henry Adams felt that the experiment, which he regarded as "the lawful outcome of Transcendentalism," glowed with "une naïveté ravissante." Ripley's plan was naive and impossible, said Adams, but ravishing and attractive to the fondest hopes of man. Adams on this score foreshadows modern historians like Arthur Schlesinger, Jr., who say of men like Ripley that they dreamed dreams of madness so that others might dream at all.[6] Although Ripley certainly did not consider himself mad, he would agree with Adams, Dall, and Schlesinger that the Brook Farm experiment, whether it achieved its major goals or not, would at least succeed in awakening his neighbors.

The motives for Brook Farm, then, were manifold. As a reaction to his age, Ripley's plan sprang from a fear of violent revolution and from a contempt for the anti-Christian values of capitalism. As a positive response to the spirit of the era, Brook Farm was but one of a series of drastic reform measures; but it exceeded others in its optimism by testing the times to see if the moment had yet arrived to create the Golden Age. As a Transcendental project, it intended to provide a means for developing self-culture within a community of like-minded souls and to present a concrete example to show the world in deeds as well as in words precisely what Transcendentalism meant. Because of the broad spectrum of motives and reasons for establishing Brook Farm, the story of Ripley's experiment, as Emerson maintained, does indeed provide "a fine historiette of the age."

II *Goals*

Throughout 1840 Ripley maintained an ambivalent relationship to his radical project. Brook Farm was his exclusive brain-child; and, like all children, it gave its parent a great deal of joy, much worry, and a considerable amount of embarrassment. He was convinced that the experiment was necessary, that Transcendentalism deserved and demanded a trial, but he wished that someone else were more willing to undertake the task. Although he hoped for success, he suspected that the project might spell financial disaster to its participants.

More than that, he was distressed that the other Transcendentalists were lukewarm to the test. Even his close friend Dr. William Ellery Channing, the one man among the older Unitarians who inspired more Transcendental projects than any other minister, was more interested in another commune. Two months before the Brook Farmers took up residence at West Roxbury, Channing wrote to encourage Adin Ballou, the apostle of non-resistance and the founder of Hopedale, saying that Ballou would fulfill at last Channing's dream of "an association in which the members, instead of preying upon one another . . . after the fashion of the world, should live together as brothers, seeking one another's elevation and spiritual growth."[7] For Ripley to have received slight encouragement from his fellow Transcendentalists must have been distressing enough, but to have it generously bestowed on other communal leaders must have been almost humiliating.

Ripley also found himself in the peculiar position of having to justify his flight from Yankee practicality to his supposedly spiritually minded friends. On a walk with Margaret Fuller on a spring day in 1840 he radiated the happiness he felt: he was so excited that he seemed reborn. Fuller quickly brought him to earth, expressed her doubts as to the practicality of his scheme, and asked why he did not go into business instead or find some safer means of promoting his views. Taken aback, Ripley defensively replied that he could not leave his calling and go into business without at least a trial with the commune. He was impatient with the artificial life of reading and writing, and he had to undertake this experiment which would be valuable for him and for the world even if it were short-lived. Fuller sympathized, but she also insisted that weeding onions was not the best way to link the Self with Nature.[8]

In the fall of the same year Ripley launched a major attack to capture Emerson's interest in the project. Since Emerson and he were the foremost leaders of the Transcendental movement at the time, Emerson's presence would insure greater support from their friends. But Ripley still sounds almost apologetic for his radicalism on November 9, 1840, when he assures Emerson that he has not lost his common sense. He insists he is a practical man who still has "a passion for being independent of the world and of every man in it." Besides this defensive tone, Ripley also adds a light, nearly puerile touch by setting the date for moving to Brook Farm on April Fool's Day. This reference was one that Emerson could hardly have missed, for the first of April had definite significance in the nineteenth century as a date for jokes and hoaxes.[9] Along with Adams, Schlesinger, and others, Ripley admitted the possibility that he might be a mad dreamer; but, if to be sane meant to dream not at all, Ripley would gladly consent to seem the fool.

The dream by November, 1840, had assumed definite proportions. Brook Farm was meant to accomplish no less than "a city of God," a "place for improving the race of men." Foreshadowing Mao Tse Tung's concept of the intellectual worker, Ripley had an even more specific objective in mind.

> Our objects . . . are to ensure a more natural union between intellectual and manual labor than now exists; to combine the thinker and the worker as far as possible, in the same individual; to guarantee the highest mental freedom by providing all with labor adapted to their tastes and talents, and securing to them the fruits of their industry; . . . and thus to prepare a society of liberal, intelligent, and cultivated persons whose relationships with each other would permit a more simple and wholesome life than can be led amidst the pressure of our competitive institutions.[10]

Emerson could hardly object to this proposal, for it was identical to the sentiments he had expressed in "The American Scholar." Specialization had severed the intellectual from the social body, isolating him from the will and desires of the people. Brook Farm would definitely permit the scholar to be in touch once again with the rest of the social body. Still, this proposal made Emerson balk. While he wished to be in touch with the social body, he recoiled at the idea of being grafted onto it. He had informed Ripley that he would join the Association if he could be "sure of compeers of the right stamp," but Ripley would not compromise on this matter.

Instead, Ripley insisted that the experiment must be more than a pastoral picnic for the Transcendental Club. Brook Farm must "be composed of various classes of men" from diverse walks of society. There was room for intellectuals and former ministers, but farmers, carpenters, mechanics, and washerwomen must also be included if the project were to be a reliable test to determine whether or not Transcendentalism was suited to all people and not merely to the intellectual. Emerson could consent to the principle that all men were equal in their basic divine nature, but Ripley was embarking on a social program of *égalité*. He was out to prove not only that men were equal in their god-like potential but that, under the right environmental conditions, all men were equally capable of realizing and fulfilling their potentials.

To match the impressiveness of Ripley's broad social intention, he envisioned his project on a grand scale of time and money, for he did not intend the experience to be a seasonal venture for summer idealists. Rather, he planned on spending "not less than two or three years" in getting settled, in gaining stability, and in discovering in a democratic way what large-scale directions Brook Farm should take. After working, living, and thinking as a band of brothers, then the Brook Farmers could crystallize and expand the experiment whose attractiveness "would win to us all whose society we should want." Hence in 1840 Ripley already envisioned Brook Farm as a plant which, under careful cultivation, would grow gradually beyond its pastoral nature and become a Socialist experiment, which in fact it did, becoming a Fourierist commune right on schedule on January 1, 1844. No hasty project or transient adventure this, since Ripley at the outset conceived that the total Transcendental test including both phases would take at least five years.

Another significant point was Ripley's conception of funding. He complained of the large sums of money being squandered on the current presidential contest between William H. Harrison and Martin Van Buren; and he suggested that, if this were a just world, a small fraction of those profligate expenditures would be more wisely spent in financing political experiments like Brook Farm. But this world was not an entirely just one; if it were, there would be no need for Brook Farms in the first place. With no sure source of funding available, Ripley cut the estimated cost of supporting ten families for one year from fifty to thirty thousand dollars and was prepared to accept money from anyone who had faith in the project. The only exception he steadfastly insisted on was rich capitalists; for, although ministers who had inherited fortunes could invest, Ripley's conscience would not permit him to accept a single penny from any wealthy person who had made his riches directly from the capitalistic system.

Money was a curious subject with the Brook Farmers. After four years of operation, the communards were unable to operate without a loss. Each year they wondered if they would make enough money to survive the next, and bankruptcy was a constant shadow, even in their brightest days. But, while the Brook Farmers obviously did not care to go broke, they had a curious dread of making too much money. Charles Lane, an early Brook Farm visitor who later joined Bronson Alcott's Fruitlands commune, staunchly asserted his glee that they had ended another year in the red. Money taints, he maintained, and to grow rich was to become corrupt.

Elizabeth Peabody, a friend of Brook Farm whose Boston bookstore was a clearinghouse for Transcendental views, provided an historical perspective to Lane's idealistic and impractical ejaculation. In *The Dial* for August, 1841, she reviewed the failure of other communes and noted the reasons: some failed from lack of funds, and some failed more greatly in that the spirit degenerated. Of the latter, the principal factors were a religious fanaticism which excluded diverse spiritual views; the unnatural breakdown of the family as the basic social unit; the lack of education which sprang from the desire to retreat from society; and, in the case of the Shakers, an excessive financial success which turned the members away from spiritual matters to making chairs. Brook Farm, she was happy to report, carefully evaded these four pitfalls. So completely did the Brook Farmers avoid the last that no member would emerge from the experience without some degree of debt.

Besides these rather sketchy goals which Ripley adumbrated in his November, 1840, letter to Emerson, he said very little about the ideals that the experiment was to achieve. Ripley's reluctance to make a public statement of the matter frustrated Peabody, and she constantly prodded him to write a moving essay about the goals of Brook Farm. Ripley's reticence was not a whim nor the product of indecision; instead, he had a specific reason for his silence which sprang from his democratic faith and his sense of pragmatism. He had already articulated his ideas in the *Discourses on the Philosophy of Religion* (1836) and in the *Christian Examiner* articles. Now Brook Farm would be the crucible in which the various classes of people would test his ideas — verify some, modify others, perhaps cancel a few. He had said his say; now others living under proper social conditions would tell him if he had been right.

Brook Farm was then a living example of his concept of "common sense" as expressed in his sermon "On Common Sense in the Affairs of Religion" (July, 1837). Ripley had to check out his idealistic impulses with the experiences of others. Foreshadowing William James' pragmatism, Ripley believed that the only valuable abstractions were those that resulted from the needs and experiences of the people. [11] If he viewed Brook Farm organically as a plant which required slow and carefully tended growth, organicism was the order of the day for the life of the Brook Farmers as well. He would not be an imperialist and tell his comrades what to think. Instead, he would be a prudent caretaker who was maintaining correct climatological conditions for other minds to grow and discover truth as it appeared to them. In living up to his concept of "common sense," Ripley applied the same principles to Brook Farm that he and Margaret Fuller had established for *The Dial.*

Together they kept the journal open to all sincere, idealistic views which resulted at times in contradictory articles. When Emerson became the chief editor in July, 1842, the tone became monothematic; and the periodical became the mouthpiece of Concord Transcendentalism.

This freedom to discover truth by one's own self was the predominant feature that distinguished Brook Farm from all other communes. John Codman, a student at the Brook Farm school, maintained that Ripley's experiment "was the only community founded in America on the principle of freedom in religion and social life." Even Merry Mount, Thomas Morton's licentious antithesis to Plymouth Colony, was censorious (as Hawthorne tells us) since it considered seriousness to be high treason. Nonetheless, the freedom at Brook Farm naturally frustrated others beside Peabody. Charles Lane grew so irritated by it that he left the community to participate in Alcott's Fruitlands in 1843, and he accused the Brook Farmers of "schoolboy dilletanteism" and a lack of spiritual sobriety.

At Fruitlands, the only other Transcendental commune, Alcott's nine-month reign was restrictive. In addition to adhering to Alcott's brand of Transcendentalism, the members were also urged to heed his eccentric dietary and health restrictions. Not only should they be vegetarians, but they should eat only certain vegetables — those that aspired toward the sun. Since Alcott had decided that an ice-water shower at daybreak was healthy for him, he insisted that all should enjoy such showers. While Brook Farm and Fruitlands were the only two experiments in Transcendental communalism, the difference in their ambience was day and night, freedom and repression, democracy and élitism.

Left to their own devices with only gentle and occasional nudges from Ripley, the members of Brook Farm developed heterogeneous ideas of what their goals were. To John Sears, the young son of a successful businessman, Transcendentalism was nothing more than the "philosophy of the Here and Now," the belief that one should seize the moment so that each nick of time exploded with experiential grandeur. Lewis Ryckman, a moving force in America's labor movement, held a more down-to-earth view: first of all, Brook Farm was primarily an economical way of life that did not make one a slave to the merchants; second, it served as a protest to the unnatural life of the crowded and competitive cities; and, third, it would eventually "build society anew on juster principles." Once the institution was self-supporting, people of all types would flock to this "eternal city" where all would be educated "to industry, goodness and justice."

As for John Codman, he stayed within the limits of the personal benefit he derived from living at Brook Farm:

> Imagine . . . the state of mind you would be in if you could feel that you were placed in a position of positive harmony with all your race; that you carried with you . . . an earthly gospel, even as the church thinks it has a heavenly gospel — a remedy for poverty, crime, outrage and overtaxed hand, heart and brain. And every night . . . you could say: "I have this day wronged no man. I have this day worked for my race, I have let all my little plans go and have worked on the grand plan that the Eternal Father has intended shall some time be completed."[12]

Whether as an Edenic state of harmony or as a militant effort to restructure society, the Brook Farmers consistently saw their goal to be, as Ripley believed, to establish "a place for improving the race of men." The nature of the improvement might differ somewhat according to each individual's perception, but all could agree that the improvement was still improvement.

The most intellectual descriptions of Brook Farm's objectives come from those who were not actually members but were closely connected with it. Orestes Brownson and Elizabeth Peabody are particularly valuable reporters for several reasons. They were at a mature age at the time of Brook Farm so their descriptions are not naively flattering. They can not be accused of writing to promote their own vested interests since they were not participants. Lastly, their reports are contemporary and run no risk of the euphoria of retrospect as do the records of Codman and Sears. In *The Dial* for January, 1842, Peabody felt that two goals were keys to Brook Farm — the development of social cooperation and "individual self-unfolding." Both were labors of love: the former, love toward man; the latter, love toward that reservoir of divinity within.

The effect of the two goals of Brook Farm would be to prove that the crowded, grasping, exasperating life of the cities was artificial: "Is there anything which exists in social or political life contrary to the soul's ideals? That thing is not eternal, but finite, saith the pure reason. It had a beginning, and so a history. What man has done, man may *undo*. 'By man came death; by man also cometh the resurrection from the dead.'"[13] Life at Brook Farm was meant to be an effort "to live a religious and moral life worthy of the name." The commune was a ship of exploration which would discover the truth and reality among the oceans of falsehood and artificiality. Brook Farm would test whether or not man was capable of loving others and loving truth.

Peabody's description of Ripley's plan rings with persuasive lines and verges on poetic rapture, but it lacks the balance of sufficient hard thinking. It is all very well to rhapsodize that "A true life, although it aims beyond the highest star is redolent of the healthy earth" and that "the lowing of cattle is the natural bass to the melody of human voice," but such paeans do little to explain why Brook Farm and not some other form of social action seemed the best to the Transcendentalists in the 1840's. While Peabody provided the imaginative delineation of Ripley's city of God, the complementary task of supplying an analytical description of its political and social necessity was taken up by Orestes Brownson.

In the *Democratic Review* for November, 1842, Brownson adapted his rigorous thinking and vigorous style to maintain that Brook Farm was the best of all possible ways to accomplish the moral, intellectual, and physical amelioration of mankind. He begins his argument with the standard complaint that existing social structures are defective and that man is capable of envisioning a better state of affairs than he has heretofore achieved. If an ideal situation can be dreamed of, then there is no reason it can not be effected. The question of how man can realize his ideals "has become, in fact, the one great, all-absorbing question of the age."

Various types of castle foundations have been recommended, and Brownson lists them in order to show why Brook Farm has the best. First, clerics and certain Transcendentalists have urged man to seek the kingdom of God first and have neglected environmental conditions and influences; this, Brownson feels, is a grave oversight. Second, others advocate a program of self-trust, self-reliance, self-control, and self-culture; "but man is not sufficient for himself." This philosophy is fine for financially independent geniuses, but it offers little either to the poor man who must work twelve hours each day or to the mass of people who are not geniuses. Third, some reformers recommend political action, but the political parties care very little for the people and favor the powerful who insure their tenure. Men should work to elect good officials, but they should not expect much from them since they can not defeat the will of the moneyed classes.

Since these three basic forms of social action are ineffective, Brownson says the only alternative is one of three kinds of Socialism — the equal distribution of capital, the abolition of private property, or communal life. The Agrarians who desire an equal division of money and property are in error because things will soon become unequal again because of the diversity of individual gifts and talents. Neither will the policy of "no property" work because there will still be quarrels among people who claim the use of the same property. Hence community or association to Brownson in 1842 seemed the most realistic and most effective means of social reform. Since society was already too large to install a just mechanism to rule the whole of society, the nation should be split into a number of commune-states. The United States of America would be comprised of relatively independent communities, a plan reminiscent of the American plan of Confederation prior to 1789.

If the many religious and ethnic communities were excepted on the grounds that they were a retreat from society, Brownson saw three basic types of political communes as possible. The followers of Robert Owen made a mistake in having property owned collectively; for, to individualistic Americans, this policy was anathema since they felt a need to have a share of their work and to receive some tangible token of their labors. Charles Fourier's complex social program was also alien to Americans because it was obsessed with external forms and was too mechanical. In contrast to Fourier's complicated scheme, the attractiveness of Ripley's plan was its naturalness: ". . . this establishment seems to be the result, not of his theorizing, but of the simple wants of his soul as a man and as a Christian." The foundation of this community was the law of brotherly love and the desire to honor all men. Ripley had incorporated the best from Robert Owen by assuring the equal distribution of profits among the workers, and he had recognized the American passion for individuality by permitting the possession of private property.

Brownson viewed Brook Farm as a variety of Transcendentalism that was distinctly different from Emerson's and Thoreau's. To say that man would become perfect if he ignored external social influences or to say with the Calvinists that man's natural state was depraved is equally erroneous. Brownson and Ripley believed that the old dichotomy between Hobbes and Rousseau — the persistent controversy that all evil sprang from either social institutions or from the heart of man — was an oversimplification. Ripley's position was much like Hawthorne's, perhaps explaining why this recluse would join a commune; for man, like Pearl of *The Scarlet Letter,* was capable of both tremendous good and terrific evil. Brook Farm would provide a social environment that would cultivate man's angelic qualities and allow his diabolical side to wither and decay. Or man's godly characteristics would increase under proper cultivation to the extent that his ignoble traits would remain small and unobtrusive. Community, then, would not destroy individuality as Robert Owen's experiments threatened and as Emerson feared; instead, the commune would provide a maximal opportunity for self-culture in concert with a body of souls intent on achieving the same general goals.

With such enthusiastic testimony from Brook Farmers and from more objective people like Brownson and Peabody, Ripley had no need to issue a public declaration of his goals. Others were handling public relations nicely, and Ripley could concentrate on promoting his principles among other reform leaders. To Adin Ballou at Hopedale, who insisted that no communal effort could last long if it were not instilled with sectarian zeal, Ripley replied in September, 1844, that Brook Farm had lasted over three years without insisting on religious exclusiveness and had therefore proved that people could handle religious freedom and did not need to be governed by tyrannical sectarianism. As long as the principles of association were humane and faithfully practiced, they did not need to be made narrow, severe, repressive, or restrictive.[14] To a leader of the communistic Skaneateles experiment, Ripley warned that the individual must not be swallowed up by the state and that "the great problem is to guarantee individualism against the masses on one hand, and the masses against the individual on the other."[15] While society made all men slaves to a select few, Skaneateles was not much of an improvement in making everyone a slave to everyone else. Ripley conceded that he might be wrong, but he believed that his association, "by identifying the interests of the many and the few, the less gifted and the highly gifted," guaranteed the "sacred personality" of each individual.

In addition to maintaining contacts with other reform leaders,

Ripley had to defend his enterprise from puzzled and somewhat suspicious souls. The social pillars of Roxbury, who began to wonder exactly what Ripley was doing only a few miles from their homes, directed a polite but searching inquiry to him. Giving them the benefit of doubt, Ripley replied.

> I welcome the extended and increasing interest which is manifested in our apparently humble enterprise as a proof that it is founded in nature and truth, and as a cheering omen of its ultimate success. Like yourself, we are seekers of universal truth. We worship only reality. We are striving to establish a mode of life which shall combine the enchantments of poetry with the facts of daily experience. This we believe can be done by a rigid adherence to justice, by fidelity to human rights, by loving and honoring man as man, by rejecting all arbitrary, factitious distinctions. We are not in the interest of any sect, party, or coterie; we have faith in the soul of man, in the universal soul of things. Trusting to the might of benignant Providence which is over all, we are here sowing in weakness a seed which will be raised in power.[16]

Ripley then stated that he and his Brook Farmers were luxuriating in the bosom of Nature in an atmosphere of freedom and tolerance and invited the Roxbury fathers to join — if they qualified.

Brook Farm meant many things to many people, but three major goals which Ripley established and fought to maintain made the association distinctive. As a special brand of Transcendentalism, it attempted to fuse a spirit of cooperation with the concept of self-culture. As a wide-scale social experiment, it incorporated various classes of people from different walks of life. As a test, Ripley maintained a rigorously inductive approach by allowing the Farm's own members to discover what goals and purposes were worth seeking in their lives. This last point makes for the complexity of Brook Farm and the difficulty of pinpointing its exact goals; but, amid the multiplicity of aims and objectives, these three major goals stand stark and clear. To Ripley's credit, the story of Brook Farm indicates that he met his basic goals.

III *Life*

In April, 1841, Ripley purchased 179 acres of acidic puddingstone for $10,500 which, as one of his cohorts remarked, was quite a lot to pay for gravel. The land was poor and better given to dairy production than cultivation, but it was no worse than any other farmland in the surrounding area. And Ripley was keen on founding his experiment precisely in that area. To sculpt a city of God in the frontier wilderness would remove Brook Farm from Eastern society and lessen its impact on the development of American civilization. Ripley wanted to locate his demonstrable alternative to capitalism in the backyard of one of America's biggest business centers. At the same time, he did not intend his venture to be an escapade in primitivism, nor did he desire his friends to transform themselves into Rousseau's "noble savages." Situated only nine miles from Boston, they could easily attend an opera or an antislavery meeting by horse and wagon, by the New Haven Railroad, or by the Charles River. The soil was not so fertile as Greenfield's, but the location was more than compensatory. Nevertheless, the Brook Farmers so worked on the soil that they had improved it to the extent that one acre of land could yield by 1844 what had formerly taken six acres.

Nor was farming their sole economic occupation. They also produced Britannic ware, oil lamps, teapots, shoes, boots, window sashes and blinds, doors, and nature books. They had a unique steam engine which they used to run a printing press to make beautifully illustrated guides to flowers and herbs as well as to print *The Harbinger,* a journal of reform. Since the communards were also actively engaged in improving the net worth of the property, they expanded the single farmhouse of 1841 into a large communal dwelling which they called the "Hive," built a new home on a hill named the "Eyrie," and another for guests called the "Pilgrim House." They constructed a combination factory and workshop for their small industry and a house designed in the unusual shape of a Maltese cross which people came to know as the "Margaret Fuller House" because she was so fond of it. Although Brook Farm was no "cave of persecution" as Emerson complained, it was certainly a hot-bed of perspiration. The Brook Farmers were so busy that they tripled the gross worth of their commune inside of three years. The 179 acres they paid $10,500 for grew to 228 acres in 1844 with an estimated value of $30,000.

Their rapid growth was also to be their downfall. In plowing their capital back into supplies, tools, buildings, and other property improvements, they followed a practice that would make any economist shudder. An enterprise that had wide financial backing or a firm capital basis could perhaps have afforded this rapid rate of expansion, but a shoe-string operation like Brook Farm could not. A single financial crisis could snap the string which is precisely what happened when on March 1, 1846, their most ambitious housing project called the "Phalanstery," in which they had invested all their capital, burned to the ground.

Even when no crisis intruded, the enterprise was a risky affair. Although they were making money by December, 1841, the income had to be spent to reward investors, pay the mortgage, and promote development. Consequently, while the gross value increased tremendously, the net receipts were in the red until the fall of 1843 when Brook Farm could show its first profit. Still, the profit never went into a substantial contingency fund, and the project would not be able to sustain a disaster. Obsessed with rapidly building the city of God, Ripley neglected to hoard funds with which to counter the Fates.

Besides the agricultural and industrial activities of the commune, the most dependable source of income and Ripley's main joy was the Brook Farm school. Ripley himself said, "We are a company of teachers. The branch of industry which we pursue as our primary object and chief means of support is teaching." [17] Ripley taught philosophy, mathematics, and astronomy; his wife taught history and modern languages; George Bradford gave literature classes; Charles A. Dana offered instruction in Greek and German; and John S. Dwight, who would become one of the prëeminent music critics in America, taught Latin and music. Ripley's sister Marianne was the genial supervisor of the school.

The tone of the school was one Ripley had advocated in 1832 in a *Christian Examiner* article in which he praised Johann Pestalozzi's Neuhof experiment. Pestalozzi, a radical innovator in his day, later influenced John Dewey, Maria Montessori, and virtually all experiments in progressive education. His ideas were perfectly suited to the Brook Farm program since they emphasized the development of self-culture in an atmosphere of kindness and free investigation, a stress remarkable for the times. Richard Dana, who later wrote *Two Years Before the Mast,* had been sent to Ripley to study because his former teacher had pulled his ear partially from his head to stop his giggling.[18]

Brook Farm stressed learning as a gay and spontaneous experience. The three-step method involved first making the students happy, then doing some activity that coincided with their cheerful mood, and finally learning some lesson from that activity. From a picnic, the class might discover itself engaged in lessons about various types of wildflowers, in a study of insects, or in the physiological process by which cows produced the milk the students drank. One student relates how everyone was excited for three days about an astronomy lesson that Ripley was going to present during a meteor shower. On the day of the lesson, not only the class but also all the Brook Farmers and some visitors from Roxbury eagerly attended to catch a glimpse through Ripley's telescope.

Besides this innovation in methodology, the school was original in its curriculum, offering a systematic program of industrial arts — possibly the first school in America to do so.[19] Even conservatives were impressed with the school and were forced to admit it was an excellent institution. Its reputation spread far beyond Massachusetts and attracted students from the South, Cuba, and the Philippines.

Although the school did accept some indigent cases, most of the pupils came because their fathers were businessmen who were tired of money-grubbing and were dissatisfied with material wealth. They wanted their children to enjoy some spiritual and educational riches before taking their places in a competitive, self-seeking culture. This phenomenon of the poor-rich businessman and the hollowness of the American materialistic dream was rampant enough to flood Brook Farm with applications, even though Ripley insisted on keeping the total number of students to thirty or so which he felt was a manageable size. At least a half dozen of these students left records of their experiences, and all attested to the fact that their schooldays were among the happiest and most fulfilling of their lives. Not one suggested that the Brook Farm school was in any way deficient.

One curious paradox shadows the school. While it was a radical educational institution run by radical Transcendentalists, it did not produce a single radical. John Sears became a gentleman farmer, Francis Barlow enjoyed fame as a Civil War general, Arthur Sumner became a prominent Massachusetts lawyer, and George Curtis won renown as the editor of *The Atlantic Monthly* and as the founder of the Curtis publishing house. While the students' stay at the school was not long enough to work drastic personality changes in businessmen's children and while radicalization was not one of the school's expressed aims, it is nevertheless strange that not one militant social reformer nor one famous intellectual emerged. All the students grew up to be fairly conventional and respectable. They looked back on their stay at Brook Farm with wonder and joy, but the school did not inspire them to launch bold endeavors of their own. Perhaps sustained radical thought must be a mature reaction against youthful orthodoxy, or so it seems when Ripley's biography is contrasted with his pupils' careers.

The school remained Brook Farm's most reliable source of income. Financial backers and markets were fickle; but tuition payments, even if fairly low for a private school, were steady. The school was one concrete success that the Farmers could proudly show to the world until the fall of 1845, which had been their most financially remunerative year, when one of the newcomers to the school showed signs of smallpox. John Allen's daughter had contracted the dread disease before entering the commune, and the Brook Farmers gave her the utmost care. They successfully prevented the disease from spreading, but the scare exceeded the threat. Some parents withdrew their children from the school; formerly eager applicants were now reticent; and the varioloid panic was the first great disaster to befall Brook Farm. Ironically, Ripley's most dependable source of income became his greatest financial setback, just as his rapid property expansion spelled the close of the experiment. His greatest successes were to bring about eventual collapse.

In addition to the thirty students, about one hundred adults constituted the working contingent, those who actually lived and worked at Brook Farm for more than one season. The experiment had reached this size by the spring of 1842, and Ripley kept this number constant. Some of this number stayed for one year or so before beginning experiments of their own. John Collins found his time useful for developing another community at Skaneateles; Charles Lane later joined Bronson Alcott in establishing Fruitlands; Isaac Hecker left Brook Farm and later founded the Paulist Fathers. Others joined because they thought the commune would be a good place to work, whether the work was manual, as with John Cheever, or literary, as with Hawthorne. Still others like Charles Dana and John Dwight hoped to persuade Ripley and the other members to convert the association into a Socialist experiment, but some, like Marianne Dwight Orvis and Ripley's wife, valued the experience as a pastoral retreat.

These five basic types — workers, projectors, picnickers, Socialists and students — did not constitute, however, the total membership of Brook Farm. Indeed, it is very difficult to compute how many sympathizers and temporary residents Ripley had. Writers like Brownson and Peabody certainly contributed much to further the project. Likewise the lectures of John Orvis, Theodore Parker, and W. H. Channing helped immensely in promoting Brook Farm's aims and principles. Then, too, those like John Sears' father who could not actually join but backed the project with money were part of Brook Farm. And the huge number of people — in one year more than four thousand — who visited for a week or two and then returned to society with the commune's activities on their minds could also be considered members. The membership of Brook Farm could be said to resemble a tree in that the solid trunk of one hundred people who were directly connected with the soil spread to thousands of leaves representing a vast number of people who were affiliated with the project in some way.

The life there was undoubtedly exuberant. Edmund Quincy, one of William Lloyd Garrison's Abolitionist circuit riders, reported his shock when the entire contingent of Brook Farmers appeared at an antislavery rally with garlands of oak leaves twined in their hair.[20] John Sears recorded his delight at peering through some branches one day and catching five staid Unitarian ministers dancing in the pine grove. When Margaret Fuller published *Women in the Nineteenth Century* in 1845, the first full-length feminist statement written by an American woman, women had enjoyed equal rights at Brook Farm for the previous four years. While America's class structure grew more and more rigid, Ripley's community practiced its egalitarian precepts to the extent that a maid from Maine, who had joined them, left because she felt awkward at being treated as an equal.[21] Brook Farmer Lewis Ryckman later insisted on working-class demands that reflected the dignity of labor and the fair distribution of wealth which Ripley had established at Brook Farm.

Not only did Ripley succeed in making many of the Transcendentalists' dreams a reality, but he managed to make it fun. The Brook Farmers led a Spartan but not somber life. Although their days were peaceful and pleasant, they were not pietistic. They had concerts, dramatizations, pageants, and picnics; they entertained each other; and they could always go to Boston for a play or lecture. One Brook Farmer summed up the sentiments of all when he said, "On the whole, again, from the social point of view, the Brook Farm experiment was eminently successful. We were happy, contented, well-off and care-free; doing a great work in the world, enthusiastic and faithful, we enjoyed every moment of every day, dominated every moment of every day by the spirit of Brook Farm."[22] Ripley himself never gushed about his successes; he merely reported that his "family" proved that man, if placed in a proper environment, would behave decently and lovingly toward his fellow man and work conscientiously to develop his inner resources.[23]

The most touted exception to this general well-being is Nathaniel Hawthorne who, arriving in the first month of the Brook Farm operation, was also the first to quit, in October of the same year. Hawthorne also holds the distinction of being the only person who sued Ripley. When he left the commune, Ripley gave him stock in the Farm to compensate for the money Hawthorne had invested. In December, 1845, Hawthorne brought legal action against Ripley and Charles Dana for five hundred thirty dollars which was to be paid in exchange for the stock. Ripley knew there was "nothing in his character to prevent [Hawthorne's] proceeding to the last extremity" to get his money.[24] Coming as this lawsuit did hard upon the smallpox scare of the previous month, Hawthorne could not have pressed his demands at a worse time. If he made good his legal claim, other creditors could also sue for money amounting to eight or nine hundred dollars.

Harsh as this law suit sounds, Hawthorne was not so scornful as might be inferred. He went to Brook Farm believing that he could work to supply room and board for himself and his fiancée, Elizabeth Peabody's sister Sophia, and spend his leisure time writing. During the spring and summer, he found that shoveling manure in the morning did not put him in the proper mood for writing romances in the evening. In the fall, he discovered that the problem ran deeper than that; for, even when there was not much work to be done, too many distractions kept him from writing. Hawthorne needed nearly total seclusion, and a commune of several hundred laughing people was not conducive to his craft. Although he never shared Ripley's dream that Brook Farm might become a model for the rejuvenation of man, his main reason for leaving lay within himself, not in Ripley's experiment. He informed

David Mack, who tried to lure him into another association, that if Brook Farm should fail, it would not be from anything "within the confines of Brook Farm, but from external circumstances."[25]

The one factor that Hawthorne mentioned as a guarantee of Brook Farm's stability was the personality of George Ripley who behaved neither as an employer nor as a master but as a colleague and fellow laborer. From all reports, Ripley enthusiastically responded to his Brook Farm environment. One visitor in the spring of 1841 told how Ripley spoke *con amore* about how he never went to bed so tired as now after working in the fields all day. His wife, too, participated enthusiastically although she had qualms about the lack of gentility.[26] But Ripley, with what one of his cohorts called "the kindest eyes in the world," maintained an atmosphere of gaiety and joy. He regaled his companions with so many puns that, while harvesting pumpkins one autumn, they awarded him the title of "Pun King."

Theodore Parker said that Ripley compared with the rest of the community reminded him of a "new and splendid locomotive dragging along a train of mud-cars."[27] But the best image for Ripley's leadership is the traditional one of shepherd. He did far more tending than pulling or tugging. Sometimes he would animate his flock's spirits through humor. Sometimes he would inspire them with example, as when the newest and poorest member of Brook Farm, William Allen, had to go to Boston. Ripley insisted on blacking his boots, exemplifying through his conduct the principle that brotherly love can overcome class barriers.[28]

The toughest responsibility Ripley faced was discipline. In spite of the freedom and minimal rules, rules were nevertheless necessary; and rule-breaking was also inevitable. Ripley's problem was how to preserve the peace and harmony of the whole without becoming authoritarian and repressive. He handled the problem admirably. To two carpenters who were irritating everyone, Ripley used an Indian technique and assigned them work on a project isolated from the group. After a few days, their disagreeability greatly diminished and the men eased back into their places in the commune.[29] The transgressors were rehabilitated without leaving any scars to impair the well-being of the community.

On another occasion Ripley employed a different strategem. A woman, notorious for interrupting lectures by impulsively shouting queer questions, came to Brook Farm one evening to hear Arthur

Brisbane speak about Fourier's Socialism. At an antislavery meeting in Boston she had proved such a nuisance that the organizers had had the police suppress her. A short way into Brisbane's speech, the woman sprang to her feet and disrupted him with her chatter; the audience immediately grew angry; and shouts of "Throw her out" arose. But Ripley instantly stood up, declared the meeting a free one, and proposed that they allow the lady her full say during a question-and-answer period. Then Brisbane could continue his speech, and the lady could never complain that the Brook Farmers did not hear her out with a great deal of attention and "even greater patience." His heavy emphasis on these last words made the audience laugh loudly: the woman had her hearing; and, immensely pleased at having had the spotlight, she soon sat down and never again disturbed a meeting held at Brook Farm.[30]

Margaret Fuller had told Emerson in 1840 that she believed Ripley's experiment might fail because Ripley was "a captain, not a conqueror"; but little did she know that Ripley did not intend to be even a captain. He refused to command, cajole, or cozen fellow members. He would not invoke rules or fall back upon his authority as the acknowledged leader to coerce people into self-culture and into proper conduct. His method was always to persuade others by his own example, to challenge misbehavior with a good-natured sally, and to offer an eye-twinkling admonishment as if from a kindly uncle who warns his nephew that he is not allowing his divine self to rule the perverse imp in his character.

Ripley's leadership was directly responsible for the success of Brook Farm's exuberant communal life. The great hopes and aspirations this Transcendentalist had for mankind, as well as "the ever bounteous joyousness of his nature [which] sparkled out in wit and mirth," was infectious. His influence was greatly responsible for the glowing accounts of the jubilant and intensely meaningful life the Brook Farmers enjoyed. During his life he was remembered fondly; and four months before his death in 1880, a former student said that he continued to be "the chiefest [*sic*] of the fixed stars" of her mind's vision and that his inspiration lived on in her four children.[31] Ripley's attitude as leader — neither captain nor conqueror, but fitting colleague to all — set the tone of the community. The "Hive" was the largest building and busy center of their projects. What Ripley said of the "Hive" was a true metaphor for Brook Farm life — there was much activity and cooperation, much humming and honey, and very little sting.

Still, Ripley did not want merely a peaceful idyll; his experiment was not meant as a pastoral retreat. Although he refused to play the role of conqueror, he meant Brook Farm to be a captivating example, one that would persuade society at large to change. Brook Farm had to become even more militant. A success for two years as a model of living Transcendentalism, Brook Farm would now become a Socialistic challenge to capitalistic America. In the fall of 1843 the Brook Farmers began to rack their brains to conceive how their commune might have an even more forceful impact, not only upon the imaginations of their countrymen, but upon the political structure of their culture.

CHAPTER 4

Brook Farm: Socialist Challenge

I *Phalanx*

TO start the New Year of 1844, Brook Farm announced its change from a Transcendental experiment to a Socialist commune with the unanimous signing of the articles of association based upon the theories of Charles Fourier. The transition was not impulsive; it sprang from many months of discussion of several issues. One major factor was that, since the Panic of 1837 was finally approaching a close in 1844, Ripley needed an even more dramatic model than the Transcendental idyll to entice Americans away from capitalism. A logical way of accomplishing this goal would be to link the heretofore isolated Brook Farm experiment with a larger political movement; and one historian estimates that America had over two-hundred thousand declared Socialists in the 1840's.[1] If Ripley could forge some formal connections with this group, he could convert his experiment's public image as an aloof body of a hundred or so Transcendentalists into an integral part of a massive social development. Brook Farm had proved the possibility of living in harmony with a great amount of individual freedom; it was now time to turn this possibility into a serious challenge of the existing social structure.

One important spur to this increased militancy was Brook Farm's old nemesis: the lack of funds. As early as December of the first year Brook Farm was making money but not enough to pay the mortgage, the loan interest, and the cost of rapid expansion and property development. In November, 1843, the commune was a going concern and for the first time ended in the black.[2] But Ripley's personal letters tell a different story. On July 22, 1843, he wrote to Minot Pratt, the most practical of the Brook Farmers, "The great evil we suffer from is one that we share with all poor men, and that must prove an obstacle in almost any situation, namely, the want of sufficient means to accomplish the ends we have in view. Hence, we work to great disadvantage; the realization of our idea is constantly thwarted by outward impediments."[3] In addition to the existing debts and expenses, Ripley felt a dire need for a large dwelling or phalanstery to ease "the restricted accommodations, the confusion and disorder" of living conditions which persistently impeded their quest for "a higher good."

The situation was aggravated by an episode that Ripley considered a base betrayal. John Collins, one of William Garrison's antislavery speakers, visited Brook Farm in 1843, showed a great interest in the experiment, and asked to see Ripley's list of outside contributors and investors. Ripley naively trusted Collins, only to discover that Collins used the list to dun Brook Farm's patrons for contributions to his own community at Skaneateles a week before Ripley approached his backers. Ripley complained that Collins had "done what is in effect the same thing as cheat us out of our money," and he denounced him publicly in a liberal periodical as a "dishonest and intriguing man."[4] Faced with the loss of his financial prop, Ripley must have looked upon the coming year with considerable apprehension. He desperately needed a replacement for the strut Collins had kicked away.

Hence, Ripley was even more open to the idea of transforming Brook Farm into a Socialist experiment. He had told Pratt that "comparatively a small sum of money would place us at ease in pecuniary matters and enable us to improve our outward life; but the want of that small sum may prove a serious, perhaps a fatal obstacle to our progress." Possibly Ripley was trying to justify his conversion to Fourierism for the un-Transcendental purpose of exploiting the capital reserves of rich Eastern liberals such as Horace Greeley, T. B. Curtis, E. G. Loring, and Marcus Spring. Hawthorne, for one, described the shift (in *The Blithedale Romance*) as an "infidelity to its own higher spirit." Orestes Brownson in 1842 called the original Brook Farm system superior to the Fourieristic plan. Many of the female Brook Farmers, including Ripley's wife, were strongly opposed to the transition throughout the experiment's life. In 1840 Samuel Osgood had found Ripley scornful of Fourierist Socialism; and in July, 1846, Marianne Dwight reported that, while Ripley was "working for a far future" along Socialist lines, he felt that Fourierist communes were not yet practicable.[5]

Hence, Ripley's love for Fourier Socialism was something less than wholehearted. He made the transition for three main reasons. If he adopted the label and made a few formal changes, he could call for new sources of revenue from the New York coffers of Marcus Spring, Horace Tweedy, and Horace Greeley. Just as practically and even more honorably, Ripley wanted to forge links with the Socialist movement in America as a whole. The third reason was that Ripley's plan had always been to allow the thoughts of his communards to brew on their own without any dictating of goals from him.

The result was a three-way split. One group, including Sophia Ripley and Pratt, preferred the status quo. Pleased on the whole with the original Brook Farm experiment and euphorically oblivious to the persistent financial crisis, they offered no new ideas and desired no substantive changes. A second group was discontented with the experiment: Emerson sarcastically called the effort a "French Revolution in miniature, an Age of Reason in a patty pan"; Charles Lane accused the Brook Farmers of "schoolboy dilettantism"; Bronson Alcott established in 1843 what he considered a true Transcendental commune called Fruitlands, one that lasted nine months.

A third group was headed by Charles Dana who replaced Minot Pratt as Ripley's righthand man after 1843. Dana had been in communication with Horace Greeley as early as August 29, 1842, when Greeley praised the Brook Farmers' aspirations, but he accused them of élitism and impracticality. "I do not deny the advantage of your plan for a community of which every member shall be actuated solely by a true Christianity or a genuine manfulness. . . . Yet can we hope to bring the world suddenly or speedily to this frame of mind? . . . Hence my fear for your system — that it is adapted only to angelic natures, and that the entrance of one serpent would be as fatal as in Eden of old." Greeley's preventive anti-toxin was Fourierism: "I think Fourier's system avoids this danger by having a rampart of exact justice behind that of philanthropy."[6]

After considering Fourierism for a year by reading Albert Brisbane's version of it, *The Social Destiny of Man* (1840), and by corresponding with Brisbane and Greeley, Dana became convinced that Fourierism was the system Brook Farm should adopt. His argument was that Fourier had the same ultimate goal of creating a

"Heaven on Earth" and that Fourierism could do so through peaceful means: "It does not so much seek to overturn the old order of things, as to supplant it; it does not tear down our rotten and creaking shelter, until its own beautiful mansion invites us to a more secure abode."[7] Fourierism, Dana claimed, did not seek to regenerate human nature, nor was it available only to angelic natures, nor did it "make war upon any part of human nature, but only upon its false circumstances and subversive conditions" through a system of "exact justice."[8]

One example of "exact justice" was the problem of labor. Initially, Ripley had counted upon people's desire for physical activity to complement study in order to get the work done, for the only injunction of Brook Farm was that its members live as fully as possible. He had hoped this physical activity would mean that the communards would find joy in farming, in constructing handicrafts, and in preparing products for market. He counted on a natural thirst for cooperation and for doing kindly favors for the good of the community to get the less desirable jobs and routine duties done.

The upshot was that a Brook Farmer might go out one day and work laboriously from sunup to sundown only to be so exhausted or so disenchanted that he would do no more work for a week. Although Ripley's colleagues might work hard, they did not work consistently; and Dana's "exact justice" would correct this fault by requiring sixty hours of weekly work from each adult with a careful record of work hours kept each day. Formerly, one had only had to demonstrate that he was living fully; and equal credit was given for an hour spent painting pictures and for one spent painting barns. Under Dana's plan, more credit would be given for effort expended on less desirable chores: one hour spent shoveling out the cow barn was equivalent to three hours at the easel. Hence, in practice, the sixty-hour week was still a humane requirement if part of that time was devoted to chores.

This seemingly practical solution to Brook Farm's main problem appealed to many of the communards. Sealing the matter was the fact that Charles Fourier's temperament was congenial to the Transcendentalists in that he believed in God, believed He was not malevolent, and believed that He had created the universe on an ordered and harmonious plan which man could discover. This emphasis on the discovery of God's laws, as opposed to the imposition of abstract ideals, lay strictly within the mainstream of the American Transcendental movement. Moreover, Brisbane's condensed 1840 version of Fourierism kept to the most practical ideas and deleted the most fanciful; and Brisbane popularized Fourierism on the front page of Greeley's *New York Tribune* beginning in 1842 and in a periodical called *The Phalanx* which he started in 1843. Fourier's faith in a divine order was balanced by his complicated and mechanical analysis of evolutionary development. His paradisiac dream of a heaven on earth was tempered by his idea that there were thirty-two phases to earth's complete history. The eighth phase, which would not dawn for thousands of years, would be one of total peace and harmony. Mankind in 1840 was in merely the fifth phase, far from achieving perfection. Hence Emerson's and Hawthorne's complaint that "Fourier had skipped no fact but one, namely Life," was not altogether fair since Fourier was clearly conscious of man's frailties and of man's low rung on the evolutionary ladder.

The thoroughness, logic, and comprehensiveness of Fourier's analysis of social relations made him attractive to Americans who envisioned a better life for mankind. The major irony was that, in spite of its many proponents, Fourierism never had a fair trial. Fourier had insisted that at least 1600 to 1800 people were necessary to complete a Phalanx (his term for a commune or association) and to fill the various occupations needed to make the Phalanx self-supporting. Brisbane lowered these minima to 400 people with $400,000 at their disposal. Even though over forty phalanxes were established, not one even approached these figures. Brook Farm lacked 300 people and $370,000. Instead of pouring money into Brook Farm and encouraging communards to go to West Roxbury, Brisbane, Greeley, and other Fourierists split their interests and capital among the North American Phalanx (1843-45) at Red Bank, New Jersey, and the Wisconsin Phalanx (1844-50) in Fond du Lac county.[9] The bane and the boon of American optimism is to have the courage to try grandiose projects which, because of inadequate support, are doomed to failure.

The transition of Brook Farm from a Transcendental experiment to a Fourierist commune consisted primarily of changes in form, whereas the original goals remained virtually the same as shown in the new constitution of January 18, 1844: "to establish the external relations of life on a basis of wisdom and purity" which meant developing an organization based upon the principles of justice and love; living in a spirit of brotherly cooperation instead of selfish competition; running a school which provided the best physical, moral, and intellectual education of children; promoting an "attractive, efficient and productive" system of industry; preventing anxiety about hunger and want; diminishing the desire for excessive accumulation; and, in general, creating a "greater freedom, simplicity, truthfulness, refinement and moral dignity" in their lives.[10]

The major change, as the constitution makes clear in the first paragraph, was that Brook Farm for two years had struck the public as a private experiment involving a hundred or so malcontents who sought to escape from society and create the best life they could for themselves. Now Brook Farm would cease being silent. The Brook Farmers welcomed public observation and sought actively to change public opinion in order to expose the weaknesses and cruelties of the capitalistic system and to supplant these with a preference for their own brand of Socialism.

The main idea they wished to promote was that wholesale reform was feasible, that people could better their lives. To broadcast this idea on a public scale, the Brook Farmers made a special point of showing up at liberal meetings en masse; and the men dressed fantastically in beards, peasant blouses, and mule-eared boots. They made a point of being noticed so that their principles could be expounded to the curious. They began publishing *The Harbinger,* a Socialist periodical which quickly became the chief organ for all reform movements. In one issue, Ripley challenged avowed liberals, "Is it not worth while . . . at least to look at a remedy which promises to eradicate absolute poverty, do away with the temptations to crime, make the executioner and constable useless functionaries, diffuse inward contentedness and peace, and thus bless the whole population?" He also insisted that Fourierism was consonant with the essentials of Christianity and was both scientifically and religiously sound.[11]

Another aspect of the new militancy was the Brook Farmers' venture on the lecture circuit. Ripley had a long, a medium, and a short speech ready to meet any call to lecture about the cause. But he could not afford to be away from the commune for too long a time; consequently, he left that task primarily to John Dwight and John Orvis. Both men's main objective was to assure America that

Socialism and association did not mean the death of individualism. Dwight went so far as to say, "that there is not and never can be Individuality, so long as there is not Association. Without true union no part can be true."[12] The Brook Farmers had indeed developed a brand of Transcendentalism which differed markedly from Emerson's self-reliant and self-contained individualism.

Perhaps the most dramatic single move the Brook Farmers made to publicize their Socialist views occurred in March, 1845. Many had scoffed at the Brook Farm idea from its inception. They accused the Transcendental intellectuals of being incompetent farmers, and they expected the project to fail within two or three years. Yearly, they had had to choke back their scorn; for, instead of going broke, the experiment seemed to burst with new, more vigorous life every year. The hordes of visitors increased annually as did the number of applicants. The expansion and improvement of property and facilities never lagged. The Brook Farmers boasted that they could produce in one acre what formerly took six acres to grow; and by November, 1843, they could point proudly to a handsome profit. In 1844 the Brook Farmers became more confident and more militant, and the major organ of radical movements, *The Harbinger,* was established on their premises. Finally, in March, 1845, Ripley administered the crowning touch by arranging for Brook Farm to be incorporated into the State of Massachusetts. No longer could he be accused of setting up a retreat upon someone's dairy farm, for the Brook Farm Association was now on the same legal footing as any township. The project looked so successful to outsiders that one merchant confided to Emerson his fear that private farmers would be forced into "association in self-defense."[13] Albert Brisbane's dream seemed imminent: an America dotted with hundreds of Fourierist communes which one day would supplant the town and city system, thereby converting America from capitalism to a mosaic of Socialist commune-states.

But this dream soon dissolved, for the spring and summer of 1845 were the penultimate seasons, and fall brought the smallpox scare which shattered the idyll and virtually closed the school. Ripley's letters and articles during the succeeding winter are a record of his frantic search for a few thousand dollars to fulfill his dream. On December 3 and 5, he begged Brisbane to ask a total of fifteen thousand dollars from Greeley, Tweedy, Spring, and other

Eastern backers to put Brook Farm back on its feet, only to learn that these men planned "the best means of bringing Brook Farm to a close" in order to devote their full interests to the North American Phalanx in New Jersey.[14] In desperate straits, Ripley broadcast a public appeal in the February 28, 1846, issue of *The Harbinger,* calling upon the American middle class to support his experiment.

This appeal amounts virtually to a public confession that Brook Farm was not capable of being a self-sustaining operation, at least given the fast rate of expansion. There was no time for the plea to be answered for on March 1, 1846, a catastrophe occurred which sealed Brook Farm's doom. Riding the crest of optimism of the summer of 1845, all the available capital and promised contributions were invested in erecting the much-needed structure called "the Phalanstery" which would be large enough to accommodate most of the Brook Farm members. On the evening of March 3, 1846, while Ripley was running the latest issue of *The Harbinger* through the presses, he heard the frightful cries of "Fire! Fire!" Rushing to the scene, he found "the Phalanstery" — his symbol of the future on which they had worked since 1844 and into which they had poured their available capital — irremediably ablaze. Though the Brook Farmers struggled mightily to contain the fire, their efforts were futile; the entire structure burned to the ground.

The reaction to this catastrophe was varied. Sophia Ripley and Marianne Dwight were delighted by the pyrotechnics and felt that they could now shuck this Socialistic nonsense and return to the idyllic life they had enjoyed. John Orvis and John Dwight made a run of the project's supporters to see if they could collect enough money to recoup their loss and continue their work. Dwight, who actually penned the experiment's most rousing epitaph in the November 7, 1846, issue of *The Harbinger,* reminded Americans of how the tremendous impulse given the whole Socialist movement "by lectures, publications, discussions, conversations has proceeded from this center." He consoled them that, "The outward hush, the incidental part has failed; but the essential *fact* survives." The ideal of Association, like Christianity, "triumphs in its failures." Although even as enthusiastic a supporter as Dwight could not dare to say that Brook Farm had demonstrated the practicality of Fourierism, he could claim that Ripley's project had proved the desire for a more humane system than capitalism.

Ripley remained strangely quiet. Observers say that he managed to be steadfast and good-humored, but this stoic exterior must have concealed an inner sadness as he witnessed the auction of greenhouse plants to pay debts, the rental of the farm to outsiders, the departure of communards when told that the farm could no longer support all of them, and the sale of his beloved library which had lined both walls of the long entrance hall of the main building. From March 4, 1846, to September, 1847, when the farm was finally sold, Ripley, his wife, sister, and a few others stayed on to run *The Harbinger* presses and to teach the few students left in their school. In clunking about the Brook Farm buildings, hearing his boots echo throughout the now empty rooms, in wandering the grounds where previously hundreds had gamboled or conversed of Transcendental matters, Ripley daily encountered the ghost town that his dream farm, the beacon meant to guide the world to a better life, had become.

With his fondness for jokes, puns, and capers, Ripley must also have been struck by the bleak humor of the situation. He had intended the experiment to be a test of Transcendental principles to see if they were viable in the real world. He had also meant that Brook Farm should test the temper of the times to see if Americans were ready to adopt bold ventures to revamp their existing sociopolitical system in order to create a more benign society. Given his scientific temperament, which had first attracted him to Fourier's rationalistic program for reform, he must have lamented the project's inconclusive results. It might have been better had Brook Farm been a clear-cut failure, for then the issues of Socialism, Transcendentalism, and Christianity would have been settled as far as Ripley was concerned. But no definite results were to be seen, and Ripley found himself in the frustrating position of a scientist whose laboratory had burned down before the experiment was finished. The trial Ripley had set up did not end with a final yes or no, but only with as many questions as there were when he had first set foot on Brook Farm soil. The fiery interruption forestalled Ripley's desire to erect exclamation points after each of his statements of principle; the only punctuation he could honestly use were ellipses and question marks.

Brook Farm continued, nevertheless, to provide much inspiration. After Ripley died in 1880, Brook Farm still had massive appeal because of, among other developments, the closing of the frontier and the Haymarket Riots. In 1897 Caroline Dall explained that "we owe the most permanent results of the Transcendental movement to the enthusiasm kindled and sustained at Brook Farm." From 1887 to 1912 Georgiana Kirby, Edith Curtis, John Codman, Lindsay Swift, and John Van Der Zee Sears found the market eager for books on Brook Farm; and many other Brook Farmers published short autobiographical accounts in magazines. On the other side of the Atlantic, Friedrich Engels, who of course felt that communes were futile and should be supplanted by Communism, said of projects like Ripley's, let "literary small-fry" ridicule Utopianists, "For ourselves, we delight in the stupendous grand thoughts and germs of thought that everywhere break out through their phantastic covering, and to which these Philistines are blind."[15]

Even today, fascination with communal life continues with a hundred communes of various sizes and goals in existence; but the most famous is Walden II which is based upon B. F. Skinner's book with *Walden II* as title. Historical communes, like those of the Shakers and Fruitlands, also report an upsurge of interest. But this concern has no resemblance to the missionary zeal of Ripley relative to Brook Farm. He had dreamed of reforming the world; the most a modern communard hopes to achieve is an oasis of serenity that will last a few years. While Ripley dreamed of supplanting capitalism without shedding blood, most modern communes seek merely to retreat from society.

At the time of Ripley's death in 1880, the issue of communes on the Brook Farm scale was dead. Mark Twain and C. D. Warner's *The Gilded Age* (1873) gave the name to the era which contrasted with Ripley's high hopes, for the novel reveals, first of all, a loss of the faith in the Golden Age that Ripley and the other Transcendentalists envisioned. Second, the book concedes the superficial appeal of American society in marked contrast to Ripley's railings against the "Iron Age" whose cruelty and selfishness had no trace of gilding.

The death of the communal dream was ironically evidenced by the rise of Utopian novels in America in the 1880's and 1890's. Edward Bellamy published his best-selling *Looking Backward* in 1888; William Dean Howells, his *Traveller from Altruria* in 1894. Other Utopian novels of the period include Byron A. Brooks's *Earth Revisited,* E. Stillman Doubleday's *Just Plain Folks,* Charles

S. Daniel's *AI: A Social Vision,* and Soloman Schindler's *Young West: A Sequel to "Looking Backward."*[16] Bellamy certainly believed in the elimination of sordid human motives, the promotion of the general welfare, and the fulfillment of each individual; but he lacked confidence in communal experiments and insisted that a reformer must stay within the system he hoped to reform. An ideal state could take place only in the far future.

Even with the economic failure of Brook Farm, Ripley did not lose faith in his principles, nor did he lose hope that drastic changes for a better society could take place in his lifetime. Approaching late middle age, burdened with debt, and with his communal dream in literal ashes about his feet, he nevertheless persisted in promulgating his views by concentrating more energy within the system as a Socialist leader, primarily through *The Harbinger,* the major voice of reform movements in America; and he still insisted on the necessity of ideal communes as models for mainstream society to emulate.

II The Harbinger

The Fourierist monthly that Albert Brisbane started in New York in October, 1843, was moved to Brook Farm early in 1845 where Ripley became the editor-in-chief and changed its name from *The Phalanx* to *The Harbinger.* The sixteen-page quarto was published weekly from June 14, 1845, to February 10, 1849; and its name, like *The Dial's,* hopefully betokened the Golden Age of truth and harmony. The journal was both literary and political. Ripley published a translation of George Sand's *Consuelo* in the first volume and of Fourier's *Cosmogony* in the second. Politically, the weekly opposed capitalism, slavery, and "this infernal war with Mexico;"[17] and it supported prison reform, labor unions, women's rights, associative Socialism, and other reforms. Frank L. Mott, the dean of nineteenth-century American magazine history, said that Ripley's journal "was vigorous and rather lively, and always high-minded."[18]

To Ripley, *The Harbinger* was a fitting successor to Brook Farm and a continuation of his reform work, perhaps even on a larger scale. In the January 16, 1847, number, he insisted that Socialism needed two things to make it work — "a voice speaking daily to the people" and a model community. Since his efforts with the phalanx had failed and since no signs indicated that a model phalanx would be built, he decided to devote himself to his publication. While the need for practical trials and public lectures was imperative, Ripley was also convinced that "A reform like that in which we are engaged, which relies on statistical facts, numerical calculations, scientific analyses, no less than on noble appeals to the sentiments and aspirations of man, demands the aid of the printed page as well as the spoken word."[19]

Before the Brook Farm fire, Ripley had announced in *The Harbinger* that he and his cohorts had accomplished several important goals. They were free of the frivolities of fashion, arbitrary restrictions, and the frenzy of competition. They had established sincere and genial relationships, personal independence, and social equality. After the fire, Ripley wrote that Brook Farm was a kind of harbinger in that it and all other reforms were a guarantee that one day Socialism would take hold; since people wanted it and needed it, they would one day have it.[20] As to the real *Harbinger,* Ripley's faith and optimism were just as strong as before the fiery demise of Brook Farm. On December 7, 1847, he wrote to John Dwight, "We have now resources to give it a place in American literature, in American history — shall I not say in the progress of Humanity — which no publication ever enjoyed before." For the pittance of five dollars a week, he poured his energies into the project, worked harder than ever, and believed he was working to better advantage. So devoted was he that he told Dwight, "I intend to kill myself if we don't make *The Harbinger* the almightiest paper that the world ever saw."

Ripley's efforts and hopes were gratified, for the periodical soon became the chief voice of all reform movements; it was respected at large both for its journalistic proficiency and its thought-provoking content. Technically, it was much admired for its clean type, accuracy of text, and regularity of publication, factors which were almost unknown to*The Dial.* As to content, the periodical had two main thrusts — the political practicality of Fourier Socialism and the philosophy that made that brand of politics preferable.

One major political idea that Ripley tried to promote was that reform within the system was not possible; but his finest single essay on this theme was "Andrew Jackson," written shortly after the President's death in 1845.[22] Ripley first praises Jackson as "the unflinching opponent of monopoly and privilege" who was elected by the common man. Ripley felt that Jackson's acts were motivated by "the genuine spirit of equality," but that his efforts were hopeless since the fundamental social principle of competition was rotten. By trying to patch the flaws in the existing social institutions in order to make them fairer instead of erecting "a new edifice on the crumbling ruins of the antique structure," this liberal President had merely helped perpetuate selfish principles and had contributed to great calamities like the Panic of 1837 and the spoils system. "It was the mending of an old garment with new cloth, — an operation which usually aggravates the difficulty which it is meant to correct." To Ripley, the election of the friends of the working man to political office and the attempt to effect minor changes in the system did little good, created none that was lasting, and could cause great harm. The entire foundation of American society had, therefore, to be revamped: "This is a work that no political reforms can effect. We need an organic change in the structure of society; the substitution of justice for fraud, of love for force. . . . Society must be made to revolve on a new pivot." One appropriate fulcrum, Ripley maintained, was Fourierist Socialism.

Specific reform movements also had Ripley's sympathies. He threw the weight of *The Harbinger* behind labor unions, one of whose leaders was John Cheever, a former Brook Farmer; and he placed labor reforms at the top of his list both because they seemed more feasible than others and because industrial reform was a prerequisite for all other reforms. In order to convert America to Socialism, some measure of control over the industrial magnates was essential.[23] The feminist movement also gained *The Harbinger's* support, although Ripley pointed out that, at associations like Brook Farm, women's rights had already been awarded and that equality had been a reality not a dream.

The more insidious issue of slavery was problematic to *The Harbinger.* Although the staff praised antislavery organizations for their fine sentiments, they had no hope that this issue would ever be solved through legislation but that the feminist and labor movements could. The only alternative was war — an issue *The Harbinger* equally opposed. Consequently, Ripley avoided this topic and only proffered Socialism as a panacea. Association would cure slavery, as well as poverty, war, and other social ills: "The axe must be laid to the root of the tree, or no universal good can be hoped for from the sincerest purposes of reform." [24]

Universality became the crux of Ripley's Socialism. He took the standard political maxim of "the greatest good for the greatest number," but he transformed it to read "the greatest good for *all.*" Was this so radical, Ripley sardonically asked? Did not the very motto on our currency promote the idea of many united in one? Associative Socialism, he believed, "is the truly consistent embodiment in practice of the professed principles of our Nation." The goal was to found a society which would "furnish every individual with the means of educating all his faculties and a sphere for their activity." On the other hand, society must be so constructed that the free play of individual talents and powers would result in the promotion of the general welfare, a society in which the individual would "find his own happiness in the common happiness and excellence of all." [25] To achieve these goals, Ripley hoped that the time was ripe for a peaceful social revolution; but he rightly suspected that his compatriots would prove too apathetic and that "the grass may grow over our graves before it will be accomplished."[26]

The real driving force behind Ripley's political position was the fear that individualism was on the wane. Although Emerson criticized Ripley for submerging the individual in the mass, Ripley actually prized individualism and sought to find a way to allow the individual to fulfill himself without allowing individualism to manifest its most deleterious social effects — selfishness, snobbery, classism, racism, and disregard for the welfare of others. In other words, Ripley tried to come to grips with the basic paradox of his society: the conflict between self and society, individualism and equality, pride and love. He felt that his system provided answers for these conflicts, for a person could be individualistic and still cooperate with others for the betterment of man. Instead of hampering individualism, he hoped his Transcendental Socialism would allow it to flourish in a humane way.

But such a development was not possible or present in the present system. One did not need to be a Socialist, a Transcendentalist, or a Fourierist to realize that the indevidual was shrinking daily, that his power was waning, for "The whole tendency of modern society is to degrade man; once there were giants on the earth; now man is dwarfed, mutilated, monstrous; absorbed in a base, petty individualism; enervated in body and mind; greedy for gain, lustful for pleasure, contemptible in selfishness; his religion mechanism, his morality mummery, his God an idol. Not for these vile ends was human nature so magnificently endowed."[27] The rise of industrialization was but one significant factor in this process, one that Ripley foresaw as only a token of the tremendous impact it would one day have. He was not opposed to machinery or to technology, but he clearly saw that, given the present state of affairs, industrialization would increasingly dehumanize the individual.[28]

In such articles Ripley came to grips with the basic dichtomy of American culture — the problem of the individual and society. He admired the Puritans for their perception of life: "Certainly, the subjection of the world to the dominion of evil."[29] But the Puritans erred in ascribing the source of evil to the individual: "A more profound view, however, shows us that the fault is not in the intrinsic elements of human nature, but in the imperfect institutions under which that nature is trained and developed." Ripley warned that one should not condemn the savage for acts that seem barbaric; his values are merely the result of his environment. Speaking more like Mark Twain and Edward Bellamy than Emerson, Ripley asserted that training and conditioning could change human actions.

In one article, he says, "Thus, the simple change of the position of an individual in the social mechanism in which he is born is sufficient to change entirely his ideas, his beliefs, his manners and habits, or in a word, his morality and his life. This no intelligent man will call into question."[30] Instead of lamenting this fact as an insoluble situation in which the individual is merely a product of society, Ripley found it a cause for hope. One only needed to make the social machinery conducive to the growth of Transcendental impulses and effect alterations "in the present order of society" which would be "favorable to the development of a high order of character." But, while Fourierism, Association, and Socialism could produce beneficent social changes, many other avenues of reform existed. As long as Ripley had control over the editorial policy of *The Harbinger,* he promised he would accept any and all articles that "in any way indicate the unity of Man with Man, with Nature, and with God." Remaining true to the principles he had formulated in *The Dial,* he insisted that "it is the duty of all persons who sincerely desire to aid in the progress of the human race, not to abandon themselves blindly to one particular doctrine, but to try all and to hold fast to that which is good."[31] In garnering a wide range of experiences and in sampling the entire gamut of theories, creeds, and systems, Ripley had faith that the Transcendental principles which had, he thought, their scientific and political expression in the Socialist writings of Fourier would be verified.

With such faith, Ripley believed he was testing his conception of the very existence of God and the character of human nature. In looking about him with Puritan eyes and in witnessing "the polluted and vulgar order of society," he could not believe that this world was the fulfillment of human destiny: "If it be so, man's whole nature is a lie and the voice of the Creator has spoken in it but to deceive."[32] That God might be a jokester who had perpetrated a cruel hoax by instilling man with a longing for a better life was an appalling thought. If this were truly the best of all possible worlds, why did man feel this driving compulsion for reform? If misery, squalor, and greed were the truths of life, how was man able to envision paradise? Either divinity and harmony were illusions, or they were valid goals toward which man must strive:

> No one can believe, who believes in the beneficence and universality of the Divine Providence, that man is doomed by his nature to such a career of crime, confusion and misery. There are too numerous, too palpable, too conclusive proofs of the goodness of the human faculties, in their intrinsic character, to allow this thought to be harbored for one moment. Man is destined to a harmonious and glorious development, . . . to present in his social relations on earth an image of the order, symmetry, and perfection with which he has endowed the hierarchies of Heaven. . . .[33]

This passage reveals the foundation of Ripley's and other Transcendentalists' great leaps of faith. Their obvious optimism is rooted in horror that cynics might be right in saying that religious ideals are lies, or that God exists as a diabolical prankster who torments man with impossible dreams. To settle for things as they are is to deny man a divine destiny; to accept life as necessarily fraught with "crime, confusion, and misery" is to scorn the urgings of the heart toward individual and social perfectability. To idealists like Ripley, the choice seemed clear between cynical acceptance and grandiose dreams; there was no middle ground. Ripley's great flights of faith were prompted by the one "thought" which must not "be harbored for one moment"; his idealist optimism was complexly interwoven with its psychological opposite. When Ripley soars highest, it is easy to lose sight of his main propellant which is fear that hollow cynicism might be the only alternative.

His experience with *The Harbinger* did much to make the

pessimism of cynics seem persuasive. For over two years while the periodical was published at Brook Farm (June 14, 1845, to October, 1847) Ripley was the sole editor-in-chief with Charles Dana and John Dwight as his political and esthetic assistants. While chief, Ripley maintained high journalistic standards and an eclectic editorial policy which echoed *The Dial.* Always leery of Transcendentalist Ripley whose Fourier Socialism stood second in importance to his Transcendental principles, the powerful Fourierist leaders seized the transfer of *The Harbinger's* headquarters to New York after the close of Brook Farm as an opportunity for demoting Ripley by making him only one of several main contributors. E. P. Allen, a capable functionary who would give the leaders no trouble, was appointed the new editor-in-chief.

Ripley mildly accepted this rebuke, swallowed his pride, and worked as diligently as he ever had in his new capacity. He and his wife took up residence in the New York suburb of Flatbush where his home and his place of work provided a geographical metaphor for his Transcendental hopes and his pessimistic suspicions. Flatbush was "a lovely romantic village — fit retiring place for a philosopher or poet," for Ripley found New York "just what I expected, slavish and shabby in the highest degree." Flatbush seemed an "oasis in the desert" and reminded him of his joyful days at Brook Farm, but New York seemed to verify Hobbes' belief that life was nasty, brutish, and short.[34] Flatbush was a token of how pleasant and wonderful life could be; New York, a dismal reminder of how harsh, squalid, petty, and miserable life was.

If only the conflict between dreams and actuality could be settled one way or the other, man's lot would be much easier. If hopelessness, want, and selfishness were the final order, then man could try to reconcile himself somehow to his condition; if idealism were heroic and not ridiculous, then a man could confidently devote himself to idealism. But the conflict could not be resolved, and the issue remained a dark mystery. Throughout his term as minister when he preached Transcendentalism, throughout his Brook Farm experiment and his efforts with *The Harbinger,* he saw some people who surrendered to cynicism and completely embraced the system. Others were willing to sacrifice all for one idealistic cause or another. Still others, by far the greatest proportion of mankind, exhibited the bifurcated, perhaps hypocritical, behavior of espousing idealistic principles while practicing vulgarity, greed, and materialism.

Advancing into middle age, Ripley was tiring of his vigorous reform efforts and of his self-sacrificing devotion to propagating Transcendental principles. Trained from youth as a scholar with a propensity for seclusion, at forty-seven he grew weary of playing the activist and of trying to alter human behavior radically, of constantly putting his idealistic beliefs to the test with such little results to show for his attempts. His personal life — illness, domestic problems, disagreements with his co-workers, and international affairs — did much to promote his feeling of weariness.

Although the economic failure of Brook Farm did not fill Ripley with despair and although his demotion on *The Harbinger* and the shabby spectacle of New York's materialism did not thwart his zeal for reform and his faith in mankind, a series of events, personal and international, dampened his enthusiasm and sapped his strength in the years 1847 and 1848. On the domestic scene, Sophia secretly converted to Roman Catholicism in 1847. This religious crisis reached a peak in 1848 when she concluded that her heart was too cold to know God. Her husband had told her that God was within; but, though her priest gave her a more conventional location, she could find Him neither within nor without; and her universe became a void. The existence of God was a certainty, but knowledge of Him was not hers. From this religious crisis of 1848 until her death in February, 1861, she was a haunting specter that daily mocked Riplley's Transcendental intimations. He could write at his desk about the unfathomable potentiality of man; but, across the room, knitting silently in her rocker, one living example negated his words. Aside from Mrs. Ripley's condition, his own physical situation worked against his spiritual promptings. His eyesight, always poor from arduous study, became worse because of his unstinting efforts on *The Harbinger.* In 1848 he suffered a prolonged illness, possibly tuberculosis, which lasted for almost two years. Early in 1849 he fell and broke his arm.

If these personal difficulties were not enough, the world situation made Ripley's cause more difficult. The year 1848 was one of European revolutions and their failure hurt the cause of American Socialism. Margaret Fuller, to whom Ripley was quite close, sent reports about the pathetic Italian Revolution, its ineffectiveness amid great hopes and sacrifice, its betrayal by internal liberal elements led by the Pope. The French Revolution was seized by American newspapers, especially the New York *Herald* and the New York

Express, as a warning example of the dangers of Socialism. Americans were persuaded that Socialist periodicals like *The Harbinger* knew not what diabolical furies they were kindling; and Ripley, powerless over the turn the global situation was taking, could only lament, ". . . *the* question of the day is — the misery of the masses is felt to reach its climax, and poor Fourierism which points out the cure must be reproached as the cause."[35]

On the American scene, the discovery of gold in January, 1848, on the other side of the continent did nothing to promote Ripley's cause. Why should Americans engage for several years in a dubious battle to reform America when one could become rich immediately by merely running a pan through a California stream? Karl Marx gloomily admitted that the revolution in America would have to be postponed because of the gold rush; and Horace Greeley, one of the staunchest American Fourierist advocates, advised young men to go West.

All in all, 1848 was a very bad year for the cause of American Socialism in general and for *The Harbinger* in particular as the principal Socialist voice. Reform interest subsided and the magazine's subscription dwindled until *The Harbinger* was threatened by bankruptcy in October, 1848. Some of the editors, and Parke Godwin the principal one among them, wanted to tone down the periodical in order to make it more palatable to the rising conservatism in America; but Ripley led a faction that staunchly opposed this proposal. He argued that to lessen the journal's militancy would be a betrayal of the principles they all espoused, and he was successful in forestalling Godwin's proposal. He also made the practical offer that the staff accept a twenty per cent reduction in salary.

Ripley worked even harder for *The Harbinger,* but its doom was sealed by the spring of 1849. In March the decision was made to turn it into a monthly and change its name to either "The New Times" or "The Spirit of the Age." But the major change was that it would be converted from a radical to a liberal paper which would emphasize its non-sectarian and non-partisan nature. Ripley had not protested strongly when his editorial policy of eclecticism was subverted in order to make *The Harbinger* a Fourierist mouthpiece, but he could not stand idly by to see its horns polled. Since he would have no share in the hypocrisy of a mild journal which paraded itself in the guise of a serious and dedicated vehicle for reform, he had no recourse but to resign.

His resignation in March, 1849, spelled not only his official separation from the four-year-old *Harbinger* but a revaluation of his reform role. After his failure with the Purchase Street Church, his abortive attempt to make Transcendentalism a militant endeavor, the collapse of Brook Farm, and now the demise of *The Harbinger,* this fourty-seven-year-old man concluded that, although the dream of a Golden Age was still valid, the dream showed no prospect of being fulfilled in the near future. In April he wrote to his close friend John S. Dwight, "I see no prospect of organizing any collective movement with the materials on hand." But, to balance this harsh conclusion, he added, ". . . still the world rolls on, and the occult designs of its Creator are preparing for consummation."[36]

When Dwight responded to Ripley, he implored him to continue his sacrifice in the interests of Transcendental Socialism; but Ripley's wholehearted enthusiasm was gone. He insisted that the time was not ripe for their kind of reform: "We can do nothing again, I am fully persuaded, and it is only spilt milk to try."[37] When Dwight, Charles Dana, other former Brook Farmers and Fourierist sympathizers gathered for a convention in Philadelphia in April — the eighth anniversary of the establishment of Brook Farm — Ripley stayed in New York where he dined with his fellow unemployed Socialist writers on soup and champagne where "precious little" was said about Fourierism and the cause in general.

Ripley's attitude at this point can be best described as weariness — not as disillusionment, pessimism, despair, nor contempt. He still kept his faith in the rightness of his beliefs, but he was finally persuaded that others, though they cared about principles, did not care enough about them at the present time to work in order to effect them. Part of his weariness was caused by his growing suspicion that the leaders were little more sincere than the masses. Ripley had known Brisbane, Greeley, and Loring only through correspondence and occasional meetings prior to October, 1847; but, after he came to New York, he worked with them daily — and their glamor evaporated. Speak as they might about the advantages of collectivism and about the beauty of disinterested love, Ripley recorded that "our brethren here . . . are savagely individual, they have never been drilled to ride in a troop, and it is no wonder if their [hobby horses] often prance and kick against each other, as well as all their neighbors."

Displeased by the age-old spectacle of radical leaders unable to agree among themselves, Ripley was troubled by the greater problem that the Socialists lacked consistency or, at least, sufficient earnestness to make the tremendous sacrifice that Ripley and others had made to accomplish their dreams. Consequently, he told Dwight, "The truth is and you can't deny it, the practical idea of cooperation, of social, aesthetic organization is wholly unknown to our friends in New York. Most of them openly avow that enlightened self-interest is the only spring to be relied on in social reform, and feel if they do not say, 'martyrdom be d---d'."[38] Ripley conceded these men might be right; but, if they were, "enlightened self-interest" could allow only moderate, partial reforms like trade unionism to be effective. Therefore, these men were inconsistent in advocating wholesale, revolutionary reform. If they sincerely desired revolution, then the reform movement was again at an impasse because few were willing to make the sacrifice required.

Since the rich and influential Socialist leaders of New York could not be depended upon, and since the masses had apparently abandoned their interest in the cause, Ripley's hook was indeed sharply barbed. Plunged deep into debt with the economic failure of Brook Farm, he had not become exactly rich by working for two years at the subsistence salary of at first five and then four dollars a week on the now defunct *Harbinger.* Left without any steady employment and with large debts, he turned to his pen to support himself, hoping he would not be forced to compromise his principles. "All I care for is a position to keep body and soul together by giving a full *quid pro quo* for all I receive, and then trust me," he assured Dwight, "for beleaguering the old castle of social wrong with not ineffectual thumps."

The spring and summer of 1849 was the most difficult period in Ripley's life. Nearly crippled by illness, beset by domestic problems, and besieged by what seemed the collapse of the movement in which he had invested so much, Ripley tried to keep body and soul together by being a "penny-a-liner" and by contributing articles written in many different styles to a wide variety of magazines, including humorous travel sketches for the Cincinnati-based *Columbian* under the pseudonym of "qui." Arduous and uncertain as these labors were, a worse alternative was tightfisted Horace Greeley's offer for him to work long hours for the *New York Daily Tribune* at very meager pay. Nevertheless, Ripley refused some work because of his pride and principles. He declined the *Christian Inquirer's* request that he rehash theology for them, he staunchly resisted going on the lecture circuit to give dull lectures about well-worn philosophies, and he adamantly refused Theodore Parker's offer that he deliver a few Sunday sermons in his church.[39]

These pressures would have broken a lesser man, and Ripley himself lamented, ". . . here I am a miserable invalid, all but a cripple, with no fruits of tough labors but disgraces and discontents."[40] But, in the same letter, his courage and undaunted Transcendental faith shone through. He said he did not feel degraded by these hard times; rather, he felt himself "still at the top of the Universe and [able to] trample on human pride." This point is crucial because many critics such as Arthur R. Schultz and Henry A. Pochmann have incorrectly said that Ripley lost his faith and that his mental growth ended when he moved to New York. Indeed, Charles Crowe asserts that after 1850 Ripley's "letters reveal a bitter disillusionment, a withdrawal from deeply felt commitments, and ultimately, a return to social conservatism."[41]

The facts contradict these assertions. It is true that at times, such as during the severest crisis of his life in 1849, Ripley's strength and energy were weakened by outside or physical forces, but his personal convictions always remained strong. While from 1849 to 1859 Ripley generally was less outspoken because he had to solve financial problems, his faith had not diminished, and his public image needs to be compared with his personal correspondence. In the middle of this difficult decade, as one example, he informed a friend in 1853,

> For my own part . . . the only religion which I believe in is the recognition of the Divine in man and nature. The Good, the Beautiful, and the True is the Holy Trinity which commands the conviction of my intellect and the adoration of my heart. . . . Hence I can love and worship all True, Good, and Beautiful men and women as incarnations of the ineffable, inconceivable Godhead. The adoption of this faith seems to me the turning-point of humanity. . . . When men receive this as a living faith . . . the millenium will dawn upon the nations, social harmony will be inaugurated, and this 'nasty' world will be transfigured into the heavenly Zion.[42]

Three years later, he told Theodore Parker, "It is always a pleasant thought to me when I reflect on how little I have brought to pass for my day and generation, that at least I have been loyal to the principles of truth and freedom. . . ."[43] Many faults can be ascribed to Ripley, but the charge that he betrayed his principles and lost his faith is an egregious error.

It is true that during the decade after *The Harbinger's* demise his writings were temporarily less militant, partly because he was spread too thin in writing for several different magazines and partly because he had to conform to editorial policies which seldom welcomed radical essays. But the major reason might have been the arrival of a decade quite unlike the previous one. When Ripley began his new career as journalist, the febrile 1840's were fast giving way to the fatuous '50's, which, as Samuel Eliot Morison says, ". . . shed a warm glow of hope and satisfaction over the American scene." A writer in the *U.S. Review* in 1853 predicted that electricity and technology would so transform life that, within half a century, "Machinery will perform all work — automata will direct them. The only task of the human race will be to make love, study and be happy." Nathaniel Hawthorne said the 1850's offered nothing "but a commonplace prosperity, in broad and simple daylight."[44] Since it seemed untimely and unprofitable to continue to rail against society when most citizens appeared satisfied with it, Ripley contented himself with a few "not ineffectual thumps" against society while he pursued a new role as a man of letters — a role that he would lead for more than half his adult life and one that won him fame, money, and respect as one of the principal intellectuals in America. His political function would be as "the loyal opposition" to mainstream America rather than the declared belligerent.

In doing so, Ripley was in step with the development of the Transcendental movement. The 1840's had been a decade of experimentation which included several attempts to test the practicality of Transcendentalism. Brook Farm had run from 1841 to 1847, *The Dial* had lasted four years, and Margaret Fuller's "Conversation Classes" and the Transcendental Club had been short but exciting experiments. In all these projects, Ripley had played an instrumental role. In addition, Bronson Alcott had tried his Fruitlands experiment in 1843, Thoreau had spent two years at Walden Pond from 1845 to 1847, and one night in jail. After this decade of a half dozen different experiments in "living Transcendentalism," the movement became exclusively literary. Instead of showing the world through dramatic demonstration how to live transcendentally, the Transcendentalists were content to inform the world through the written word.

CHAPTER 5

The Man of Letters

I *The Cyclops and the* Tribune

BY predilection and training an intellectual, Ripley was now free to devote himself to scholarly interests. He would hereafter speak about reform issues only when society showed a willingness to listen. He hoped that as a Man of Letters he could do much to give birth to that willingness.

For the last half of his adult life, then, from 1850 to 1880, Ripley practiced daily the multiple functions of literary critic, political commentator, newspaper philosopher, and popularizer of the newest scientific and psychological discoveries. In short, he was a Man of Letters, a role that Ripley helped establish in America and that lasted until the days of H. L. Mencken. In a sense, this position was a continuation of Ripley's desire to be a "Minister to the people." His academic and scholarly credentials were sound, his intelligence indisputable, his humanitarian impulses proven, and the people were eager to hear this man's interpretation of events and ideas. They listened to him in the Protestant tradition wherein they gave him an attentive and appreciative hearing because of the respect he had earned, but they reserved the right to disagree. To listen was especially easy now that Ripley had filed away his labels as a Transcendentalist, Fourierist, and Socialist and spoke to them only through the persona, if persona it may be called, of Man Thinking.

The role of the Man of Letters has faded from the American scene. The reason is partly due to occupational specialization. Knowledge has become so vast that a man today can only aspire to an expertise in a narrow sub-field of one branch of human knowledge. When a modern scientist, the biologist Loren Eiseley for example, attempts to bridge the gap between the two cultures and comment upon philosophy, philosophers and biologists alike suspect the wisdom of stepping outside one's specialization. In Ripley's day, this attempt was considered admirable, not suspect. It was only proper for a man who had mastered one field to speculate on others.

Indeed, to Ripley's mind, this attempt was not only possible but necessary. As he confided to a friend in 1852, he still had hopes of accomplishing ". . . a grand comprehensive reconciliation — Moses, Job, Christ, Plato, Rousseau, Jonathan Edwards, Charles Fourier, and I don't know who of the Germans, — united in one glorious synthesis. . . ."[1] Although he disagreed with Emerson about many points, he did concur with one requirement of "The American Scholar": in order to comment profoundly on the general nature of mankind, the intellectual had to be informed about all the main areas of serious human inquiry. Hence, while extrapolating for others the latest scientific and literary experiments in a cogent and clear manner, he was also tending to his own growth by garnering a variety of information which might allow him new and profound insights into the mystery of man.

Ripley enjoyed being a "minister to the people" in an era when that role was highly esteemed. Contemporary reviewers vied to outdo each other in praising him: the *Hartford Courant* in 1872 rendered its "considered judgment" that Ripley was the ablest critic in the country; the *Springfield Republican* lauded him as the best journalist in America; and publications as diverse as the New York *Evening Gazette,* the Chicago *Daily Tribune,* and the *Atlantic Monthly* praised him almost without reservation. So overwhelming was the contemporary evaluation of his service that at least one modern historian considers Ripley to have been for nearly thirty years "both the arbiter of taste and intellect for many educated Americans, and the oracle of culture for a mass audience."[2]

Ripley earned this praise primarily with his *New York Daily Tribune* articles which mount into the thousands and which, among other matters, established the first regular column of literary criticism in America. These efforts were buttressed by other independent projects, for he helped found *Harper's Magazine* in 1850 and contributed to it intermittently until his death. In 1852 he and Bayard Taylor published a *Handbook of Literature and the Fine Arts* which was well received. He was so pleased with this project that in July, 1862, Ripley conceived another anthology "Books and Men: A Series of Critical and Biographical Sketches" which, according to the preface, would be "a modest guide to the popular mind in the judgment of 'Books and Men' that called forth a general public interest." But this project was aborted, partly because Ripley became absorbed in another project, one that proved immensely popular — the publication from 1859 to 1862 of the sixteen volumes of the *New American Cyclopaedia.*

An overall view of Ripley's vast editorial projects discovers a pattern which parallels what took place at Brook Farm. Ripley began his commune with a small group of friends which soon expanded to include a wide variety of classes, and his cyclopaedia projects reveal a steadily strengthening affinity to the popular mind. In 1838 he had published *Specimens of Foreign Standard Literature* which was meant for an élite cadre of American intellectuals who were interested in the newest Continental philosophical movements. In 1852 his scope was broader, and the *Handbook on Literature and the Fine Arts* was intended for a group of individuals concerned about esthetics. With the *New American Cyclopaedia* in 1862, however, Ripley covered all subjects from esthetics to zoology; and his audience included all literate people and not just esthetes, theologians, or philosophers.

While the tendency to address himself more and more to the popular mind in his cyclopaedias reflects the pattern of Brook Farm, the economic result was dramatically different. The 1862 *Cyclopaedia* gained Ripley and the other editors between $40,000 and $45,000 — a fortune in those days — and the project was so popular that Ripley published a new edition in 1873. Ironically, some of the Brook Farm backers, remembering their twenty-year-old debts, dunned Ripley for free copies of his *Cyclopaedia* to compensate for their losses in his Socialist experiment.

The success of the *Cyclopaedia* is easily understandable since it maintained standards of excellence in a day when the market was glutted with shoddy and biased productions. George Willis Cooke claims that Ripley's "was the first competent work of the kind published in this country, and has been surpassed by no other in critical ability and scholarly insight."[3] Since Ripley wanted and secured the most competent writers he could find, his project, though popular, was controversial. The section on Socialism was written by Karl Marx; and since the article on Roman Catholicism declined to kowtow to the usual diatribes against popery, it elicited outraged responses from Protestants who branded the article's objectivity as biased. Although Emerson, Dr. C.T. Jackson, and R.H. Dana decided to "vehemently insist" on canceling the article about anesthesia, still a controversial subject in 1858, Ripley stood by his contributors and refused to delete it.[4]

Ripley was adamant on this score for several reasons. In the first place, he wanted to remain true to the principle he had established on *The Dial* and *The Harbinger* — that an expert should have a free hand in expressing his views unhampered by editorial policy. Indeed, Ripley saw the role of the editor as a defender of this right against attacks from outside forces, not as a censor of opinions that conflicted with the overall tone of the publication. At the other extreme, Ripley took his obligation toward his readers seriously. In one review for the *Tribune* he called the editor an "accoucheur" or midwife who did not merely explain subjects with scientific objectivity but arranged the articles to provoke thought and inspire an understanding of the subject in a new way.[5] Hence, he chose Karl Marx instead of Arthur Brisbane to write on Socialism because, although Brisbane's credentials were sound and his reputation widely known in America, Marx could present a fresh insight and burnish the reader's thought. In short, Ripley wanted articles that, in addition to giving an objective recapitulation and description of the subject, would be prescriptive and forward-looking as well.

Hence, in the 1860's while his country was being torn apart by the Civil War, Ripley enjoyed the most secure and profitable period of his life. With Brook Farm, he had shown himself capable of the most glorious dreams; with the *Cyclopaedia,* he proved he was likewise capable of being a shrewd Yankee and amassing a great fortune if he so desired. He had struck friendships with nearly all the literary and social lights of the day and had won the nation's respect as an intellectual guide. He was rich, famous, and esteemed. In twelve years he had struggled from the most difficult time of his life to the most comfortable one.

And a struggle it was indeed! In 1849-50, he slaved as "a penny-a-liner," painfully conscious that he was not producing his best work for, as he said, "a lion does not appear well at a menagerie." He was forced to write on everything from Edgar Allan Poe's writings to Louis Kossuth's battles to Emerson's lectures to recent ship arrivals and departures. He had to make his name by contributing to a wide variety of magazines from Western ones like the Cincinnati *Columbian* and the New Orleans *Picayune* to Southern periodicals like the *Charleston Literary Gazette* and the *Southern Literary Messenger,* to obscure magazines like the *Galaxy, Arthur's Home Gazette,* and the *Manchester Examiner,* as well as famous Eastern publications like *Harper's, Putnam's,* the *Washingtonian,* the New York *Quarterly,* and the New York *Ledger.* At a penny a line, he did not become rich, especially since his Brook Farm debts had to be paid. Moreover, while the conservatives distrusted him as a Socialist and Socialists distrusted him as a Transcendentalist, he had to prove that he had the energy and the popular appeal to be accepted as a Man of Letters.

From among this wide variety of newspapers and magazines, one would arise which would be the primary vehicle for Ripley's views and the principal guarantee of his fame. Even more than his editorial projects, more than *Harper's,* and more than any of his other critical contributions, Ripley's name became synonymous with *The New York Daily Tribune* to the extent that more than one rival newspaper cited Ripley above Horace Greeley as the dominant reason for the *Tribune's* success.[6] But Ripley's relationship with the *Tribune* was at the outset ambivalent. On one hand, he admired the *Tribune* since, with its readership of well over a half million, it was one of the most influential papers in America. Moreover, Ripley liked its lofty aims and history of reform commitments. Greeley had thrown his lot in with the party of the future and progress, and Ripley could readily abide that gesture.

But the *Tribune's* inherent defect was that, since it sought to be simultaneously a popular newspaper and a champion of reform, it ran the risk of being hypocritical. Karl Marx had said to Engels that ". . . under the guise of Sismondian philanthropic socialist anti-industrialism they represent the . . . industrial bourgeoisie of America. This also explains the secret why the *Tribune* in spite of all its 'isms' and socialistic humbug can be the 'leading journal' in the U.S."[7] The *Tribune* was thus no *Harbinger,* but *The Harbinger* and other radical magazines had failed. From the staff of the *Tribune* Ripley could find a certain degree of tolerance for his radical viewpoints; and he could also be sure that his opinions appeared in a publication respected for its high journalistic quality and its wide circulation.

The major disadvantage of the *Tribune* was the editor-in-chief himself. Even genial George Ripley found Horace Greeley a hard man to live with. To John S. Dwight, Ripley said Greeley's "prejudices stick to him like a burr. Greeley is a hard case personally, and as coarse, sharp and gritty as a flint. . . . I don't believe he would go across the street to save any of us from hell-fire, — Charles [A. Dana, now a fellow *Tribune* editor] himself not excepted."[8] Ripley's prognosis was accurate; for, a few years later when Dana refused Greeley's edict that Marx be fired as a regular contributor, Dana himself was fired.

But, in the spring of 1849, Ripley's situation looked "a lot like starvation." He was tired of squandering his talents over a dozen or so periodicals and wanted to concentrate his efforts on one. Since the *Tribune* was the most influential of the lot, he had to accommodate Greeley's idiosyncrasies if he wanted a full-time position. In March, he accepted the paltry sum of twelve dollars for seven nights a week. By July, he was writing all the book reviews; and, by September, he was officially considered a regular full-time staff member. In July, 1850, Margaret Fuller, the first full-time literary critic in America who had gone to Europe to cover the Italian Revolution and also, perhaps, to escape Greeley, died in a tragic shipwreck while returning home; and Ripley was promoted to his friend's position.

By 1850 Ripley was securely installed, therefore, as the specialist on all manner of literature for the most influential newspaper in America; and, during the next thirty years, he strove to prove himself the Man of Letters *sans pareil.* His domain included everything printed in book form — science, philosophy, psychology, children's stories, history, maps, reform pamphlets, modern and Classical literature. An investigation of three of these broad categories — politics, philosophy, and literature — presents a comprehensive understanding of his ideas and developing trends of thought.

II *Politics*

In the nine years before 1850 Ripley had been actively at the forefront of every major political and intellectual development. In his present capacity of Man of Letters, he found himself defending, promoting, and championing causes led by others, not by himself. His function was to support the movements of labor, education, women's rights, Abolition, and Socialism in order to encourage the friends and to excoriate the enemies of progress. His role was now that of a vigorous patron of reform rather than that of a militant participant; and, as such, a re-ordering of priorities took place. In 1841 he had broken with Emerson; he had insisted that thinking alone was not sufficient for — action too was necessary. Meditation must be married to militancy, and the Brook Farm experiment was the immediate upshot. In 1852, although still valuing the man of action as a great man, Ripley placed him below the level of the poet and the philosopher who concerned themselves with discovering eternal and universal truths instead of dealing with specific problems of the moment.

In 1852 Daniel Webster, the Golden Orator, died; and the press competed to publish the most laudable tributes to America's famous statesman. Refusing to be pulled into the hysterical whirlwind of panegyric, Ripley considered Webster "the great high-priest of the practical understanding" and labeled him a "man who deals with facts and events and exhausts his intellect in acting on their relations." He insisted that such a man, valuable though his contributions be, was inferior to the poet and philosopher and to the idealistic reformer. Other writers credited Webster with having saved the union through his support of the Compromise of 1850, but Ripley recognized his efforts as temporary patchwork which did not effect any permanent correction of social problems.[9]

Other conservative personalities fared differently with Ripley according to the degree of honesty they showed. Hypocrisy was the one quality that would provoke Ripley into rage. If he suspected a writer of fakery or trickery, he would let out all the stops in a bitter diatribe. Conversely, if the writer was frank and sincere, he would repay in kind, even if the man's opinion was antithetical to Ripley's own. In this regard, even P. T. Barnum fared much better than Moses Stuart, Ripley's old enemy from the Norton-Ripley controversy. Barnum was tolerable, even enjoyable, because he was "so blatant a humbug" that he nearly had the word "JOKE written across his forehead." But Stuart's fakery was malicious, sinister, and insidious. When he tried to argue in his book *Conscience and The Constitution* that slavery was constitutionally sound, Ripley stridently condemned him for a hypocrisy which dedicated the church to God and the chapel to Satan. "No one conversant with the productions of this author will be surprised to find in it a medley of egotism, pedantry, garrulism, . . . argument and puerile anecdotes, with the entire absence of congruity, coherence, or good taste." On the other hand, Ripley offered a fair and impartial review of Richard Hildreth's Federalist interpretation of *The History of the United States* because Hildreth's politics were clear. He was conservative and was probably wrong in his views; but, since he was consistent and not hypocritical, he received liberal treatment from Ripley.[10]

Sincerity and frankness were the bywords also for Ripley's appraisals of leftist writers. He recommended Henry Stanton's book on reforms and reformers because it had much valuable advice and information for the reader, but he blasted the author for his rhetorical pretension. Stanton's heart was in the right place, and his ideas were valid, but his prolix and convoluted style could not be excused. A reform writer must speak plainly so that his language will not give the semblance of obscurity or hypocrisy. Ripley spoke out even more harshly against a widely popular book by George Barrow called *L'Avengro,* for, besides its lack of coherence, Ripley despised the book for its two-faced nature. Barrow was an example of the clever hack writer who capitalized on the reform movement without having anything to say. *L'Avengro* pretended to be cutting, ruthless, and iconoclastic when in reality it offered "no radical ideas to frighten people from their propriety."[11] Ripley would not tolerate hypocrisy whether from the right or from the left.

As to specific reforms, Ripley performed religiously his role as a champion. He defended Horace Mann's educational reforms from Charles Bristed by arraigning the latter as a conservative defender of American aristocracy who possessed a morbid personality, a "pretentious insolence and imbecility." A few months later he recommended an educational system of Elizabeth Peabody's which was even more radical than Mann's.[12] To the labor union movement he gave his undivided sympathy and support; and he even called upon literary men to align their efforts with the cause of the working man.[13] On the issue of women's rights Ripley supplied much encouragement and criticism; and he chastised Catherine Beecher for advocating a haphazard program of education and pamphleteering as a "grand panacea" for male chauvinism. He praised Elizabeth Oakes for beautiful sentiments like "liberty is the divinest need of the human soul," but he faulted her for a lack of specific suggestions. In addition to fine poetic descriptions of the need for equality, the cause of women's rights desperately required some concrete and practical proposals. Three that Ripley offered were that the laws be changed so that women would be permitted to own and inherit money and property, be allowed to vote, and be granted equal work opportunity.[14]

The one cause that consumed Ripley's interest more than any other was antislavery. To his credit, he saw that the question of slavery involved more than an economic dimension and was inextricably involved with racism — a far more insidious problem. Racism probed deeply into the national consciousness and, unlike slavery, was not merely a political nor an economic issue. To attempt to understand the problem, he delved into his culture's past to discover slavery's first signs. Looking back to the inception of America, he praised the Puritans for being so shocked when James Smith brought and sold two Africans in New England that they passed a law in 1645 which forced slavers to return Africans to Africa.[15] Ripley lauded the Puritans for not endorsing slavery, and he appreciated this anecdote since it indicated that the idea of slavery was inherently abominable, at least when initially considered.

But the issue was not this simple for, as Ripley noted, while the Puritans abhorred Black slavery, they soon acclimated themselves to the practice of Red slavery. While they passed laws insisting that Africans be returned to their homeland (a law that was easily circumvented), they felt no compunction about enslaving Indians with rum. Hence, while the Puritans could be said to have been members of the first official antislavery movement, they were still guilty of considering people of a different color as their inferiors, which allowed them to practice their own brand of indigenous slavery.

Looking at a later point in American history, Ripley noted the same racial problem that resulted in the gulf between the high ideals of the American Revolution and the inequities that were allowed to flourish. He highlighted the "contrast between the political mission of America and certain inconsistent features of her social organization."[16] He lamented the inconsistency of penning "all men are created equal" while allowing the institution of slavery to remain legal. He correctly foresaw that America suffered from a schizophrenia of idealism and racism and would be racked by such an inconsistency for many years to come.

Ripley hoped that the American people would resolve this dichotomy in favor of idealism. He used the *Tribune* as a pulpit to remind people of their better natures, their lofty principles, and their idealistic tradition. He praised George Bancroft's historical interpretation which maintained that mankind as a species was motivated by a burning desire for freedom and perfection which would be achieved if people could resist the shackles of materialism and selfishness. Where he lauded Gerrit Smith, an Abolitionist and a close personal friend of John Brown, Ripley equated him with Moses, Jefferson, and Fourier. He defended Charles Sumner's antislavery position from attacks, including even some that came from "O," another *Tribune* writer.

In 1856 Ripley was "so absorbed in political interests" that he had room to "think of scarcely anything else." Contrary to *Tribune* policy, he supported John Fremont in the 1856 presidential campaign as the candidate of the new Republican party because of Fremont's opposition to slavery. If Ripley was disheartened to see the people choose James Buchanan, a former Federalist and a pro-slavery Democrat, they did not choose the third-party candidate, Millard Fillmore and his Know-Nothing party.[17] Evidently the American people chose to avoid, not resolve, the schizophrenic extremes by settling for a compromise. This compromise, of course, turned destructive; for the nation was soon engulfed in what would become the most costly debacle in its history.

Ripley, like the other Transcendentalists, had mixed feelings about the Civil War — on one hand, deploring killing and conscription, on the other, applauding the war as a necessary means of eliminating slavery. If war could repair this most serious flaw in the American social fabric, then they welcomed it so that the removal of this glaring injustice would permit Americans to concentrate on creating an heroic age. But Ripley's enthusiasm for the war was less than Parker's or Emerson's; and he said little about it, largely because he was plagued with personal problems. In June, 1860, he went to Greenfield to attend the funeral of his only brother, Franklin. Upon his return to New York, Sophia told him she had to undergo surgery for a hard lump in her breast which she had sustained in a fall the previous year against a table. The operation seemed a success; a postoperative vacation in Boston lightened Sophia's spirit; however, she collapsed soon after; and Ripley nursed her twenty-four hours a day until her death in February, 1861. She was buried at Ripley's old Purchase Street Church, which had become a Catholic parish.

At the outbreak of the war Ripley was completely alone except for one close relative — his sister Marianne who had been his major support during the early days of Brook Farm. But the war took away even this last support; for Marianne, who showed such an intense patriotic concern that Ripley deemed it "a morbid interest," was so despondent about the defeat of the Union forces at Bull Run that she took to her bed and scarcely ever left it. Ripley began 1861 by nursing his wife until her death; he ended the year doing the same for his sister. His personal grief and his familial duties were so great that it took him two years to recover, during which he had little time or energy to devote to other people's woes. Not until April 18, 1863, did Ripley feel that his sorrows had subsided enough for him to enjoy life and to work to improve the quality of life in general.[18]

When Ripley finally commented on the war, President Abraham Lincoln had declared at last that the issue was emancipation. Ripley still said little, perhaps because he suspected that emancipation by proclamation would not eliminate racism. As a Transcendentalist, he knew that political decrees would not produce meaningful social change; only improvement of the human heart could accomplish that. Yet he did support Octavius B. Frothingham's response to the New York Reign of Terror, a week of riots from July 12 to July 19 when the poor Irish whites rebelled against the draft. Ripley seconded Frothingham's resolution that this was a war for the "working-classes, a war for the free condition of *human nature.*" He attacked writers who claimed that the war was over States' rights and not slavery; at one point, he asserted that the title of J. T. Headley's *The Great Rebellion* was "a flagrant misnomer" and that the book itself, since it tried to rationalize the inhumanity of slavery, was "biased, colored, inaccurate and premature."[19]

But, in spite of Ripley's great personal grief, in spite of his less than optimistic hopes for the Civil War, and in spite of his financial success with the *Cyclopaedia,* Ripley did not lose sight of his reform principles. Some claim he lost faith and gradually settled into conservatism, but the support for this theory is slim and fragmentary. Declining to attend a meeting of communards in Maine in 1852, Ripley asked his friends "to drink to the old Archon's health in the best that your Maine-ical laws permit." In 1869 he expressed the idea that lasting social change involved a slow and gradual development as opposed to a sudden alteration. Also, he insisted that "the integrity of society depends at last not on institutions but on the integrity of individual members."[20] Such statements might imply that Ripley was shifting into Emerson's brand of Transcendentalism, but to think this is to be blind to the context of Ripley's entire writings and to ignore the impact he continued to have on the Socialist movement in America. On the occasion of his death, for example, one radical magazine touted him as "the greatest of Fourierist writers. . . . He will be remembered by the socialists of the future as one of their earliest and wisest standard bearers."[21]

Indeed, Ripley's writings indicate that his politics became even more radical as he aged. In 1851 he remained unquestionably a Socialist; for he demanded that society follow "the divine laws of Harmony as opposed to selfish competition"; insisted that Socialism did not destroy individualism; and accused those who claimed it did as being the staunchest defenders of existing political, religious, and social institutions which already squelched individualism. Nor would he have any truck with halfway measures. When Alphonse de Lamartine praised England's conservative Christian Socialism as a panacea for social ills, Ripley called his book a "flimsy, sentimental, moralizing" which obstructed the natural evolution of humanity.[22]

In the late 1870's when political corruption was at its zenith and when people seemed most apathetic, Ripley did not lose faith. Using water imagery that could have come straight out of Whitman's *Democratic Vistas* (1871), he affirmed that "The depths of a nation's heart are not to be judged by the froth which comes to the surface. The vices and frivolities of social life, like the flippant lectures of half-educated materialists, are but as ripples that disturb the surface of the water, while the strong current of common sense, morality, and religion flows on uninterruptedly below."[23] His faith in the people remained strong, and he adopted Marx's concept of the inevitability of drastic social change. Ripley insisted that America was a class society, and that the only way America could avoid class conflict was to remove class barriers, which, ironically, would be itself another form of Socialism.[24]

Ripley leaned so far to the left that he publicized the views of the most radical branch of Socialism. In 1878 he noted that the Communists in America were small in number but that they should be listened to objectively because their purported goals of "Union,

Independence, God and Humanity" were worthwhile aims. Looking abroad, he correctly charted the future of Russia. To Ripley, czarism, as a consolidation of the state, was a necessary historical stage; but "the time for a new evolution has arrived." The consciousness of the people would gradually be elevated "like the great process of nature in the epochs of creation." After this slow and careful development of consciousness, a new spirit would burst forth: "Silently and unseen it will penetrate all the fibers of the people; when a deep heaving commotion will complete the change and shake the national foundations from their accustomed place. The old decayed, and worn out elements will be swept away in the storm, which will be succeeded by new forms of beauty and life. Such a social revolution is imminent for Russia. . . ."[25] If nothing else, Ripley's Socialistic training and passion permitted him to predict accurately a great historical change in the history of the world. To accuse him of forsaking his political beliefs is to misinterpret grossly his writings.

To assess Ripley's contributions to politics and reform as a Man of Letters, the most intellectually honest position to take is that he used the columns of the *Tribune* to educate the people about their condition and about how to improve it. In the 1840's he had established what he hoped would be a rallying point around which the masses would unite to change society. When the people did not flock to his banner, Ripley, preferring to think that the people, not his principles, were in error, believed a long process of political education was necessary. As a Man of Letters, he strove for thirty years to awaken his countrymen, hoping that he might so inspire them that they would one day rally to a standard representing widespread and meaningful reform. His specific banners were women's rights, labor unions, antislavery, education, and most of all, Socialism.

III *Philosophy*

Just as Ripley's political interests increased rather than declined, his fondness for philosophy became a passion. In the last years of his life this seventy-six-year-old man would waken, dart out of bed, and light a lamp in order to jot down some notes on his new ideas. In his *Tribune* articles, he wrote five-thousand-word essays elucidating the major aspects and finer points of philosophers like his old friends Victor Cousin and Emanuel Swedenborg; old adversaries like John Locke, William Paley, and John Stuart Mill; philosophers little known in America such as Arthur Schopenhauer, Auguste Comte, and Eduard von Hartmann; and scientists with a philosophical bent such as T. H. Huxley, Charles Darwin, Herbert Spencer, and Alexander von Humboldt.

Amid this array of essays about various types of philosophy, two ideas are paramount in Ripley's thought and provide unity to his sundry statements. He felt the need for a synthesis that would work inductively from an idea or feeling and not deductively from any particular philosophical point of view. Such a synthesis would call for an application of scientific methodology to the study of human psychology, one which would focus on the mind in a rational and scientific way and not concentrate upon emphasizing any particular system. The other emphasis was, of course, Transcendentalism. In these last thirty years of his life Ripley's brand of Transcendentalism underwent a subtle shift from a search for the best means to develop the divine in man to a study of the mind as pure force and will. His Transcendental philosophy led him to probe the nature of the unconscious. Together, these two emphases, on synthesis and on Transcendentalism, make Ripley, if not a forerunner, then at least a harbinger of the exciting new theories of William James.

To his friend Theodore Parker, who expressed worry over Ripley's religious directions, Ripley confided in 1852 that he was still a Christian in the sense that Christ was a "Universal Man" and that "God in Humanity" was his motto. The church he belonged to was "The Church of the Future" whose primary aim was to achieve "a grand comprehensive reconciliation"[26] of different religions and philosophies; and the impetus for this drive was the increase of specialization which, as already observed, gave men less chance each year to understand the major trends and discoveries in all fields of human knowledge. The function of a Man of Letters was becoming increasingly difficult, the role might soon become anachronistic, and he sought to circumvent this development by focusing on the generalized philosophy of eclecticism. He explained that there were four main philosophical systems — the sensationalism of Locke, Paley, and Mill; the idealism of Plato and Emerson; the skepticism of Hume and Voltaire; and the mysticism of Swedenborg. All of these systems reflected respective faculties of the mind; for each person had a little of Locke, Plato, Voltaire, and Swedenborg in his psychology. Philosophers in each of the four systems had provided a service by analyzing the workings of each of these faculties, but each system was limited since not holistic. Each system had a grain of truth, but was fragmentary, partial; and, if it excluded the other three systems, each one was erroneous. "A perfect philosophy must combine the elements of truth involved in each system."[27] In emphasizing these aspects of Cousin's eclecticism, Ripley was clearly anticipating Max Wertheim's gestalt psychology and John C. Smut's holism which came to full flower in the twentieth century.

Where Ripley supersedes Cousin and points to William James is in his attempt not only to reconcile the four main systems of philosophy but also to link the discursive, speculative inquiries of philosophy with the methodology and analytical procedures of physical science. Ripley attempted to wed philosophy and science, speculation and analysis, the deductive and the inductive methods. The exciting new scientific discoveries never failed to stimulate him. In a letter to George Bancroft, Ripley fairly shouted, "Have you read Professor Tyndall's very curious book on the Philosophy of Heat? What immense strides physical science is making!" But the scientists who most fascinated Ripley were not those who merely explained why the sky is blue or how heat radiates, but those whose discoveries helped shed light on the nature of man and mind. Consequently, his search for synthesis focused on men like Joseph Cook, Alexander von Humboldt, T. H. Huxley, and Herbert Spencer.[28]

Ripley thrilled to Joseph Cook's style because "He so deftly combines fancies and facts that you are at a loss to determine whether you are listening to the dreams of a poet or the reasonings of a philosopher." For his thought, Ripley had both praise and blame. He liked Cook's idea that "the organic phenomena of the Universe are the result, not of mechanism, but of life" because it reinforced Ripley's own emphasis on the mind instead of external reality. He also appreciated Cook's affirmation of the "DIVINE IMMANENCY IN ALL NATURE, and of the Divine Transcendency beyond it." But, when Cook argued that the miracle of Christ's birth may be likened to a fatherless insect birth, Ripley drew the line and cited Cook as an example of what can happen to a brilliant man when he is so carried away with his own cleverness that he perverts his genius into performing mental gymnastics over trivial, pointless ideas.

Alexander von Humboldt, whom Poe praises in *Eureka,* won some of Ripley's admiration for seeking unity between man, God, and nature; he gained more of it for seeking unity in both a scientific and idealistic manner; and he won his greatest respect for indicating the limitations of human knowledge. Humboldt verified Ripley's belief that all sensuous perceptions could not be resolved into the unity of one sole idea of Nature and that a combination of all human faculties was essential in order to make sense of the world.

The one scientist whom Ripley exalted more than any other was Herbert Spencer, Charles Darwin's most popular disciple. Ripley called Spencer a "preeminent thinker and artistic writer" who combined the conciseness of Hobbes, the flow of Locke, the philosophical simplicity and earnestness of Bishop Butler, and the profundity of Kant without Kant's diffuseness and obscurity. Ripley enthusiastically welcomed the theory of Darwin, T. H. Huxley, and Spencer that man descended from apes because that theory implied that the cause of human vice was not an irrevocable part of man's nature but mere atavistic tendencies. Instead of man's being damned with a vicious nature about which he could do nothing, man's selfishness and greed were throwbacks to an earlier, undeveloped stage which he might some day outgrow. Hence, Ripley was joyful that the Golden Age which he had posited as an article of faith since the 1830's received scientific reinforcement from the theory of evolution.

In his enthusiasm Ripley called for a study of all animal conduct, especially of those living creatures who have a direct link with the ascent of man. He believed that the cooperative principle would be regarded as an advanced stage of human development. Mutual injury and hindrance which arose from selfishness would become a temporary phase preceding social relations furthered by a spirit of "cooperation and mutual aid." In such a scheme, value judgments like "good" and "bad" would no longer be based on artificial constructs or on idle dreams of the way life should be. Instead, "good" and "bad" would be "associated with acts which obstruct their [individuals'] complete living." Brook Farm had been "good" since it had sought to permit the maximum development of each individual. Even egotism, in this scheme, could be seen as a mere preamble to altruism; for the self, once its inner-directedness was completely satiated, would strive for a greater sense of gratification by doing beneficial things for others.

Far from fearing the enthronement of science as the monarch of thought, Ripley welcomed it as the harbinger of the Golden Age and as the yea-sayer of the potentiality of mankind. Indeed, the latest scientific theories of the 1870's directly caused a renewal of his faith in Transcendentalism: his Brook Farm experiment could now be called "good" on a scientific basis of cooperation. His 1836 analysis of the Bi-Part Soul of man in the *Discourses of Philosophy* found an echo in Spencer's theories. The divine quest for life as it *could be,* which Ripley had elucidated in 1836, could be stated even more positively as life as it *will be.* The Transcendental Seer, then, was not envisioning dreams of some Platonic supersensual realm; he was experiencing visions of the future that were produced by turning to evolutionary principles that actually existed within his being.

In addition to being an apparent justification of his Transcendental beliefs, Ripley thought that science was fighting the same battle against the materialists. When Elliott Coues, for example, attacked Newton's theories about the attraction of matter by saying that it would be more profitable to emphasize force, Ripley saw a parallel to his own conflicts with Locke in philosophy and with Paley in religion.[29] If reality could be split into mind, matter, and the relationship between the two, Ripley felt it more fruitful to stress the mind and its relationships. In beginning to emphasize force and relationships, science seemed analogous to Transcendental emphases.

In promoting Transcendentalism anew, Ripley's first step was to destroy all notions that equated it with a mysticism which located man's divinity in some supernatural pool of inspiration. This equation was so common that Greeley, knowing Ripley was a Transcendentalist, often assigned him to cover the latest supernatural crazes. One of these was the "Rochester Rappings," a pair of sisters who traveled about the country for two years demonstrating how they could at will make spirits rap on tables and walls. Another supernaturalist was Andrew Jackson Davis, the "Poughkeepsie Seer" who would transcribe elaborate messages from the spirit world.[30] Ripley maintained that what Davis and the Rochester girls were talking about was something quite different from what he and Emerson were saying, and he advocated a "modest skepticism" about the veracity of these events. Even if true, the truths were incidental because these messages could tell no more than what man could discover by communing with his own soul.

W. E. Channing is to Ripley a better Transcendentalist than Emanuel Swedenborg because he "presents the intuitions of his own mind, while Swedenborg reports his supposed conversations with Angels." Yet Ripley had defended Swedenborg's most famous American disciple, Henry James, Sr., since the *Harbinger* days when subscribers urged Ripley to censure James for his atheism. But his "atheism" was precisely the basis for Ripley's admiration of him; for, since James recognized that man was "the only spiritual being we know" and was the "true Divine end in Creation," Ripley felt they were at one.[31] Norton's charges about the heresy of Ripley during the 1839 controversy were accurate; for Ripley supported a religion without a god — a god, that is, in the shape of an externally located figurehead.

Some scholars have said that theologically Ripley was far more moderate than Theodore Parker, but the Ripley-Parker correspondence proves otherwise. In a letter to Parker on September 26, 1853 (Massachusetts Historical Society), Ripley took his closest friend to task:

> "Now, my dearest Theodore, it seems to me that you . . . take your stand too exclusively on the personality of the Godhead. God is Spirit; hence not Person. . . . to most men God is as much a fetish as he was to the Jews or Pagans — they place a shapeless idol more or less refined in place of the Eternal Trinity — Goodness, Beauty and Truth. . . . Here let me say you deviate from the path of true progress. The vital problem of the age is to bring man to self-consciousness — to initiate in him the knowledge of divine humanity. Everything that we ascribe to God lives in the Soul of Man.

Whitman would publish *Leaves of Grass* in 1855, and concepts like "divine humanity" and "self-consciousness" make the poet and Ripley so close in their thinking that Ripley might be considered closer to Whitman than to Parker, relative, at least, to the nature of God. But myriad differences remain between Whitman and Ripley, and the chief difference is Ripley's insistence on a teleological interpretation of existence, that man must strive to build up the "city of God" on earth. To create that New Zion, man needed to study his own divinity, which meant that he must intensely scrutinize the workings of his own psychology.

While Ripley was fighting the Spiritualists on one front — Davis, the Rochester girls, and his fellow Transcendentalists like Swedenborg and Parker — he battled the rearguard action of the materialists. Ripley, in fact, saw the Spiritualists and the materialists as twin sides of one coin in that they both argued that divinity lay somewhere outside man's soul. The Spiritualists made goodness the province of God, and the materialists explained morality in terms of cause-and-effect social relationships. Both views were anathema to Ripley. He rejected the entire eighteenth century as having suffered from a "blank Materialism." He renewed his attacks on John Locke and William Paley, but praised Jonathan Edwards and W. E. Channing for saving America by keeping alive the faith in a power above the senses and in an inherent will to do good which transcended cause-and-effect explanations. [32]

The whole history of philosophy, Ripley felt, could be viewed as a dialogue between these two antithetical beliefs: Man as machine or Man as God. He lauded Edwards and Channing for speaking stridently as minority voices to prevent the complete hegemony of mechanistic philosophy, and he was also pleased in the 1870's to see the purely mechanistic attitude lose ground.[33] Although the work of Edwards, Channing, Emerson, and himself had not been in vain, one man loomed a threat: Auguste Comte's Positivist philosophy that was immensely popular ran counter to many Transcendental precepts. Ripley admitted that his ideas were some of the "most significant intellectual products of the age," but he insisted that Comte's philosophy was not so great nor so original as many supposed. Since Comte "resolutely ignores the spiritual side of man and shuts philosophy up in the mere realm of sense," Ripley thought that Lockeans and other mechanists will "easily adopt Comte's positivism" for it offers little that is new.

To Ripley, Comte's major defect was that he failed to discriminate between knowledge and belief and hence produced a dysfunctional philosophy which ignored the holistic operation of human psychology. "*Knowledge* is the summation of all information received through the senses. *Belief,* while incorporating sense experience, includes ideas which are not rooted in *Knowledge* but which we know are true because our intuition affirms our faith in them." Ripley argued that such concepts as the soul, equality, brotherhood, God (not as a personality but as "a purely ideal being"), and the Golden Age are non-sensible in that they cannot be explained adequately as resulting from man's external relations with life. Positivism was a philosophical fragment which described only the superficial, sensual, and external function of human psychology and ignored its subconscious depths. "The sole way of escape," Ripley insisted, "is through the hated door of Transcendentalism. Comte or Kant . . . is the only alternative. Transcendentalism affirms an order of Ideas beyond the impression of the senses, — declares the reality and potency of Reason, explains and legitimates its laws, defines its conceptions, and thus founds a rational psychology on the basis of experience."[34]

The "rational psychology" that Ripley called Transcendentalism was a far cry from the early Transcendental strivings which sometimes lapsed into paeans of hope and into celebrations of vague dreams and wishes. Indeed, the rational psychology went beyond Kant and provided a point of view that reconciled the intuitive system of Kant and the experience system of John Stuart Mill, Herbert Spencer, and Auguste Comte. This new possibility which Ripley was first beginning to grasp in 1878 might indicate, he felt, "a new departure in philosophy." When publishers begged Ripley for a history of the rise of Transcendentalism, he had made a working outline, written some preliminary drafts of the section about Andrews Norton, but had soon tired of the task: he had no interest in rehashing old points. Recapitulation was monotonous, unproductive, and, worst of all, distracted him from his present studies of new trends in psychology. As he told his friend George Bancroft in 1878, now that he had much leisure due to the financial success of the *Cyclopaedia,* he was returning "with alacrity to my ancient studies, plunging deep in the current German philosophy, especially of [Arthur] Schopenhauer and [Eduard von] Hartmann."[35]

The issue that attracted and absorbed Ripley was the relationship between the Will and the Unconscious. His intensive studies in this area, which included over one hundred pages of notes, placed him in the forefront of psychological investigation which would culminate in America in the writings of William James. The first law Ripley established was that "Each form of life must be considered in its own newness and organic completeness." An organism must be studied in terms of its uniqueness and not according to preconceived patterns or expectations. This idea, which had been articulated by Goethe nearly a hundred years before and in America by Margaret Fuller, was hardly new; but Ripley's originality lay in his concept of "organic completeness." Since an organism's qualities are not autonomous and since they depend upon mental perception of them, Ripley's emphasis is not upon the mind nor the organism as static entities but upon the process between the two in the act of perception and evaluation. Kant's limitation was that he often described the mind as an independent and stable entity, but Ripley felt the mind was vibrant, fluctuating, and fluid. Whereas Kant's Pure Reason was presented much as an object under study in a closed laboratory experiment, Ripley's mind as "consciousness" depended on outward stimuli and varied in response to these stimuli. An orange, for example, had no color in itself but produced that perception in the mind. The mind does not see the perception; it sees the orange. But consciousness is aware of the color, a perception which is constantly changing from yellow to orange to brown to black depending upon the intensity and angle of light and upon the ripening of the orange.[36] The influence of Schleiermacher, the founder of phenomenology, upon Ripley can be seen to be great.

This quality of consciousness — of being aware of perception, of knowing the ever-changing workings of the mind — distinguished human psychology from the rest of creation. Instincts in animals and the heliotropic "will" of plants indicated that "Nature is pervaded with the principle of Intelligence of equal extent and certainty as the Law of Gravitation." A simple seed has such an unconscious "will" to grow that, if planted upside down, its shoot and its root will still correctly discover their proper courses. Man possesses this aspect of the Will — "an unconscious power" — and he also possesses the ability to gain consciousness of his unconscious will and drives. Awakened from sleep one night by violently striking his hand against the headboard of his bed, Ripley became conscious "that I had been dreaming of a horse who put his nose in my way, to which I gave a heavy blow. Hence I learn: 1) that I may dream unconsciously; 2) that upon awakening and becoming conscious I may remember the dream; 3) that I may exercise an act of the will (striking a horse's nose) without any consciousness of the same: but may remember the act on becoming conscious; 4) hence in a state of consciousness I may remember what has taken place in a state of unconsciousness."[37] The duty of modern psychology, then, was to study the realm of experience which takes place before the awakening of consciousness. The most crucial field of intellectual investigation was the unconscious acts and motivations of man which occurred prior to consciousness but which could be rendered to consciousness. A fertile ground for such study, Ripley recommended, is the phenomena of "infant unconscious life . . . which has never to my knowledge been thoroughly explored."

These ideas clearly indicate that Ripley anticipated by several years the pragmatism of William James and Charles S. Peirce as well as the foci of Freudian and Jungian psychology. His emphases on a rigorous and scientific study of the mind; on the importance of flow, process, and fluctuating workings of the consciousness; and on the crucial necessity of investigating the mysterious but fathomable unconsciousness — all place him in the vanguard of psychological movements which were soon to be born. His special brand of Transcendentalism served him not as a fossilized faith but as a growing intellectual attitude which allowed him to persist in the forefront of intellectual development.

But Ripley's contribution in this vein should not be exaggerated; for his notes, though ample and fascinating, remain notes. He did not develop them into an orderly public presentation of a new philosophy. While personally fulfilling and while potentially influential, his "rational psychology" remained in scattered sheets of unpublished papers. If he had had the time and the vigor to develop his new ideas, Ripley's role in the advance of psychology might have been great. As it was, when he died in 1880, his career stood truncated. To say that of a seventy-eight-year-old man, however, is considerable testimony to the vitality and power of his mind.

IV *Literature*

As the first American to publish literary reviews on a regular basis, Ripley wrote during exciting times. Beginning his career in 1849, he lived through the richest half-decade of American writing which is known today as the American Renaissance. At the start of Ripley's vocation, Romanticism was the order of the day; and poetry was considered the queen of the genres. By the end of his reign, the esthetic vogue had shifted from Romanticism to Realism; and the novel had supplanted poetry as the most vital and respected literary form. The world of literature from 1849 to 1880 underwent, therefore, vast and rapid changes. Simply to keep step with, much less promote, these developments was a severe test of the Man of Letters' resources.

To complicate matters, the relative newness of Ripley's role of literary critic as well as its monumental demands posed a problem. Not only did Ripley have to review a wide range of books from *How to Get, Keep and Spend Money* to Henry James' latest novel, not only were German, French, English, and American literary endeavors considered within his purlieu, not only did he have to publish critical appraisals of works that arrived from the presses, but he also had to decide exactly how a person becomes a regular literary critic especially since in the early phase of his office no formal models existed for this function. What primarily distinguished his role from that of former critics was the question of his audience. Since the people who read his reviews in *Harper's, Putnam's Magazine,* and *The New York Tribune* had only a general education with respect to esthetic matters he could not afford, for example, the luxury of being a Samuel Taylor Coleridge and of leading highly cultivated minds through the intricacies of a *Biographia Literaria.* On the other hand, Margaret Fuller, his predecessor on the *Tribune,* had established high principles of literary criticism which admirably transcended the bulk of contemporary reviewers who, by and large, offered personal visceral reactions to literary works which all too often resulted in mere puffs of praise or damning diatribes. Ripley maintained Fuller's tradition of excellence, but his pride would not permit him to follow docilely in her footsteps. He had to create, therefore, his own example of how one serves as literary guide to the masses.

In terms of the critic's obligation to the writer, Ripley's critical function was somewhat clearer. His model here was Charles Sainte-Beuve (1804-1869), known today as "the father of modern French criticism." Ripley honored Sainte-Beuve for establishing the revelation of the artist's soul and the work's social import as the predominant criteria for evaluating literature. But, most of all, Ripley esteemed Sainte-Beuve for being a "sympathetic critic" who strove to encourage and to assist writers in their creations.[38] This kind of critic is precisely the one Hawthorne praised in his preface to *The Marble Faun* (1860), ". . . that one congenial friend . . . in all respects closer and kinder than a brother, — that all-sympathetic critic, in short, [to] whom an author . . . implicitly makes his appeal whenever he is conscious of having done his best."

To such artists seriously attempting their best, Ripley played the avuncular role conscientiously whether the writer was Hawthorne fulfilling his great genius or E. A. Oakes striving to excel in spite of her lesser gifts. What did it matter if William Morris did not measure up to a Keats or a Chaucer? Here is *Jason,* "a poem fresh and sweet and masterly, greatly to be enjoyed . . . of trained skill, of exquisite perception. Shall we refuse to enjoy one kind of beauty because it may not be another?" To Ripley, it was absurd to attempt to measure Shakespeare, "The Child of Nature," and Tennyson, "the offspring of culture," by the same standard,[39] and it was futile since these two giants achieved greatness in very different ways. Hence, since a new literary work was not to be judged according to preconceived models or criteria, each piece of literature had to be evaluated by Ripley on the basis of what the writer attempted to accomplish in that specific work.

This critical geniality allowed Ripley to make impartial appraisals of a wide variety of literary works, but, it also raised two crucial problems. In the first place, he did not wish to lose all sense of discrimination by praising all literary efforts no matter how glib or how minor in intention. He would brook no fraud which tried to pass off hack work as serious literature, nor could he state that Hawthorne and Oakes were on the same level simply because each had tried his best. Moreover, one lion might not deserve the public's adulation as much as another. Second, Ripley believed that a critic was not solely responsible to the author's intention but that he had to bring certain esthetic expectations to bear upon a work of art. These expectations had to be general enough to permit enjoyment of a wide variety of works and clear enough to cultivate literary excellence. These twin dangers of a loss of discrimination and a lack of esthetic expectations were the Scylla and Charybdis which Ripley strove to avoid.

His comments on the novel illustrate how successfully he managed the first dilemma. He used the appeal of poor literature to castigate his readers for their inhumanity and capriciousness. The "appalling popularity" of Ouida's (Marie de la Ramée's) novels, especially her first, *Under Two Flags,* was readily apparent to Ripley: "Now like all good Americans, our heart goes out to an aristocrat. The cheerful spectacle of the elevation of a class at the cost of the painful degradation of the multitude thrills us with delight and fills us with a profound and satisfying sense of the fitness of things." Since Ouida catered to the public's weaker, unheroic natures, she could not earn Ripley's esteem as a serious writer; and he spared no effort in vilifying her works.

The vast success of books like Elizabeth Wetherell's *Wide, Wide World* highlighted another of Ripley's favorite targets of human weakness. Such books had no artistic merit, presented no gripping tale, nor did they even cater to sensationalism. How, then, did the critic account for their popularity? The answer all too clearly lay in their tone of idyllic pathos, in their quaint stereotypical characters, and in their morals. Second only to Ripley's chagrin over the public's favoring counter-progressive literature was his anger over the popularity of novels that were prized for their soporific effect.[40] Thus, Ripley easily isolated novels that were not "serious" if they were narcissistic or narcotic. If narratives appealed to man's undemocratic and unbrotherly impulses or if their goal were to lull the readers into a mindless pleasantry, they bore the brunt of Ripley's fury.

With the more difficult task of discriminating among "serious" novels, Ripley's focus was the work, both its virtues and faults, instead of a criticism of the reader or the writer. He advised Charles Dickens not to listen to *Blackwood's Magazine* which urged him to return to the unmixed mirth and pure humor of the Boz sketches. Ripley felt Dickens's latest accomplishments such as *Hard Times* (1854) and *Little Dorritt* (1857) were the best because their intention was "not merely to amuse and beguile the reader . . . but to illustrate by example some great political or social principle." Nonetheless, Ripley believed his novels still suffered from various flaws because Dickens was too fond of little Nells and maudlin Pauls; he mistook melodramatic effects for tragic intensity; his plots lacked construction and were too protracted; and his morality was commonplace and therefore false in that "he seems to suppose an unlimited distribution of plum pudding the noblest human virtue." Worst of all, his characters, besides often being gratuitous, were caricatures and not representations of real people.[41]

This adverse view of Dickens contributed to Ripley's enthusiasm about the novels of William Makepeace Thackeray. That he admired Thackeray so strongly is something of a surprise; for, as Transcendental Ripley clearly saw, Thackeray had "but a slender faith in human virtue" and anticipated "no brilliant successes from the longings of the world." But Ripley could wink at this lack of Transcendental faith since the chief novelistic goal was a Realistic portrayal of life and not necessarily an inspiration to nobler levels of human conduct. The characters of Thackeray's *Arthur Pendennis* were "likenesses drawn from nature and not arbitrarily created"; *Henry Esmond* was admirable for "its quiet wisdom and genuine beauty"; and virtually all Thackeray's novels displayed the "depths of the human heart" which, even though probed with "such truly surgical nonchalance," proffered "a profound experience of life."

Hence Thackeray fulfilled for Ripley the chief responsibility of the novelist — he managed to imbue his works with an air of genuineness, and his readers felt that real characters were embroiled in actual life situations. Unlike Dickens's novels, Thackeray's works seemed genuine, not contrived nor artificial. Indeed, since Ripley connected the discovery of truth with the development of goodness, he felt that genuineness in itself was a kind of morality, the most sincere and influential kind possible. Since the truth of Thackeray's novels was healthful and strengthening, "not flattering to human pride but crushing out all conceit and nonsense," his works "administer a bracing medicine to the effeminacy of the age, and must exert a wholesome influence."[42] To portray life as it is, Ripley believed, is to plant the seeds of human progress. Dickens had created an enchanting world with fascinating though irrelevant characters, but Thackeray had created novels that revealed human nature.

If Thackeray had any shortcomings, it was, thought Ripley, authorial intrusion. The novelist in creating genuineness and in revealing truth had to work insidiously so that his influence would have the maximum effect: "The novelist should never do anything to cause a recognition of his personal existence. He is the invisible agent that moves the magic machinery. . . ."[43] The import of the novelist's work has the greatest effect when working subtly on the reader's imagination as it is wholeheartedly engaged in the experience of the story. Thackeray erred in reminding the reader of the author's presence, for this action dulled the subtle shaping power of his art. On this score, Ripley cited George Eliot and George Sand as more successful novelists than Thackeray.[44]

But Ripley's ranking of novelists is not so important as the esthetic qualities that he prized in evaluating literature. Unlike many literary critics of the time who saw literary genres as various branches of poesy, Ripley felt that the functions of these genres were distinctly different. The realm of poetry, for example, stressed earnest self-questioning and a deep penetration of personal emotions; but the function of drama and the novel was to investigate the complex relationships of individuals in society. Even though the functions of prose and poetry were dissimilar, their ultimate aim was identical — "a recognition of the living heart beneath human forms; a longing after the perfect ideal of humanity."[45] These two goals were, however, quite different in character. "Recognition of the human heart" implies an analytical description of human nature stripped of artificial façades, but "longing after the perfect ideal of humanity" suggests an intuitive claim, born of experience and observation, of the greatest hopes and possibilities of mankind. Ripley did not believe these two goals were at odds since the conscientious pursuit of the truth of the human heart would yield valid prescriptions for alleviating mankind's weary soul and anxious social condition.

The two essential components for achieving these esthetic goals were genius and genuineness in the writer. By "genius," Ripley meant chiefly that the poet probes deeply into his personal wealth of inner experience. The man of genius may describe superficial emotions, but he does so only to give contrast to the powerful feelings which are the proper domain of genius. Although he is a Promethean figure who sees farther into the future and deeper into the soul than other men, the literary genius must also present his insights in an original way so that his vision seems distinctive. He must not only see but must move others, and he cannot do so if he uses trite images, worn-out phrases, or stale expressions. His language must seem new and exciting. The originality and freshness of his language should work to wake others to his personal discovery of a "deep inner experience" which is universally relevant to mankind.[46]

On the other hand, the literary genius must not be so original that his poetry loses a sense of genuineness or the ability to communicate. His poetry must sound distinctive but not idiosyncratic;

original, but not queer. Since his most important task is to communicate his vision to others in such a way that his vision seems sincere, he must beware of creating a language that is so new that no one can decode it. In short, the artist must work upon the body of literary tradition to create new forms. He does not create a linguistic world to which only he has access. Clearly Ripley's esthetic reflects his political and philosophical theories, for he always distrusted the ideal that was not anchored in broad human experience. Just as his political objectives were to create new forms from old ones, he wanted poets who could rework traditional literary modes into new creations.

As Ripley looked about him, he found few poets who could fulfill his esthetic demands. The most popular poets in America were still the Brahmins of the genteel tradition. Carefully avoiding an outright condemnation of these revered writers, Ripley nevertheless made it clear that he thought them capable of neither genius nor genuineness. The "fastidiously well-chosen words" of Longfellow lacked any imaginative fire: his language was smooth and bland; pleasant, not profound. His ideas were not only superficial but fake, and he ignored the anxieties and problems which plagued his perceptive countrymen. The truth of the matter was that the course of America by no means ran "as smooth and equable as these smoothly-flowing verses." Like the poetry of Longfellow, that of Oliver Wendell Holmes and of Philip Freneau was likewise hollow. The "easy, playful tone" of their poems betrayed a desire to skirt any deep inner experience rather than plunge into one.[47] Readers of these poets could pride themselves on actually reading poetry but know all the while that they would never be startled into thought or threatened with growth.

Of all the popular American poets, only John Greenleaf Whittier fared well with Ripley to whom the poet's genuineness seemed a hallmark of nearly all his poems. Whittier was close to the common mind, he identified with its interests, and he expressed many of its noblest thoughts. Although his deep sincerity could not be questioned and satisfied part of Ripley's esthetic ideal, Whittier is still not a great artist. While his hostility to wrong and his sympathy with the interests of humanity were genuine, his poetry lacked any sign of genius. This lack is not so grave as its converse; Heinrich Heine's genius, for example, created a magnificent poetic world which, immense as it is, few men could enter. Whittier speaks to the people, but does not plunge to the core of existence. Heine plunges, but the pool he dives into is cut off from the ocean of human experience.[48]

One American poet who also came close to Ripley's ideal was Frederick Goddard Tuckerman. His ideas were "thoughtful and suggestive" and clearly came from "his own experience and not from his studies or recollections." His style, too, was sound in that it did not seem "inflated, forced or artificial." But his weakness was a fondness for "unnecessary inversions" and the use of "unheard of and unattractive words and phrases." In trying to be original, he too often lapsed into cuteness; and such flaws caused the reader to suspect Tuckerman of viewing poetry as a plaything to demonstrate his cleverness rather than an influential instrument for affecting human feelings and beliefs.[49]

Finding no practicing poet who fulfilled completely his two demands of genius and genuineness, Ripley despaired. In America, Walt Whitman clearly demonstrated genius; and Ripley admired his "lusty healthfulness and rugged charms of natural expression." He praised the "sinewy strength" and "aboriginal might" of his poems, but he believed that the sensuality and radical form would prevent America from appreciating Whitman for many years to come. Tennyson and Browning were, therefore, more successful since they combined in a more influential manner power and calm, vigor and charm.[50] Great as were Tennyson and Browning, they still were not Ripley's ideal poets. His usual reference to them was mild praise such as "Browning is one of the best moderns" and "Tennyson is the finest poet of our era."

Only once did Ripley grow ecstatic over a poet, a minor poet by the name of Edwin Arnold whose eight-volume *Light of Asia* (1879) introduced Westerners to his firsthand experience with Buddhism. Ripley bruited the poem for its theme was central to contemporary philosophy, and its keynote was "the evolution of character from an exclusive devotion to self to a tender charity for our kind " — the primary issue at stake in the theories of Spencer and Comte. Moreover, Arnold's style had "all the charms of a fascinating narrative and the enchantments of a melodious verse." *Light of Asia* theoretically excelled in style and substance, form and matter; and it was, therefore, "a magnificent work of imagination, a sublime appeal in the interests of the loftiest human virtue."Ripley tendered the poem "the sincerest welcome and grasped the author by the hand as a genuine prophet of the soul."[51]

That Ripley awarded highest praise to a decidedly mediocre poetic work requires some explanation. Like Emerson, he had created an ideal that no poet fulfilled completely. In the last year of his life after reviewing thousands of poems, Ripley despaired of ever finding a poet who realized his ideal. Consequently, he grasped *Light of Asia* like a drowning man at a straw and exaggerated the poem's significance. In terms of accomplishing both goals of genius and genuineness, the most successful literary genre was prose, not poetry, a reversal of the literary hierarchy of the first half of the nineteenth century. Ripley's criticism of fiction is therefore more successful than his appraisals of poetry.

To investigate Ripley's prose criticism which spans two continents over a period of thirty years would produce a study of his most diffuse focus. A selective focus on American writers — taking the Transcendentalists first, then discussing Poe, Melville, and Hawthorne, and concluding with the Realistic movement — provides, however, a representative sampling. Ripley had witnessed Emerson's meteoric rise to a position where Transcendentalism was equated with Emersonian thought. Although he was a genial and open-minded man, Ripley could not avoid feeling some jealousy over Emerson's success. In his private letters to friends, he often confided his glee over incidents that would so embarrass Emerson that he would have to "lower his topsails a foot or so." When Parker asked to do the article on Emerson for the *Cyclopaedia*, Ripley told him that there were "many better and greater men" for Parker to handle.[52]

But, while Ripley revealed his rivalry privately, his public statements were full of objective praise. Resolutely adhering to his esthetic principles, he had to concede that Emerson was the finest essayist America had produced. His genius was truly great, for he managed to combine his visions of the ideal with his perception of reality, and be never permitted one aspect to be divorced from the other. "In the loftiest flights of his imagination, he never loses his hold on the solid earth." He did not skim the surface, but plunged down into the hidden depths of the soul; and he brought forth the greatest mysteries of mankind. If at times he seemed obscure, Ripley insisted that it was not because his words lacked meaning but because the suggestive quality of his essays and poems so subtly delineated his "lofty conceptions of the human soul." In addition to genius, Emerson evinced genuineness to Ripley. The tone of honesty and the absence of pretension were unmistakable. His rejection of all "varnish, gilding, and foppery" was total. Ripley believed Emerson's vision was distinctive and gave the reader a clear impression that Emerson saw with his own eyes and not through someone else's spectacles. Moreover, his style was robust and original in that he established a new form of the essay "to which the elegant commonplaces of Addison or the solemn platitudes of Johnson can show no parallel."

But, in spite of the fact that Emerson satisfied both Ripley's crucial esthetic qualities of genius and genuineness, Ripley had some grave reservations based not on personal rivalry but on philosophical differences. In the first place, Emerson's style was "unscientific"; and he lacked a thorough and comprehensible development of his ideas. Often what he said in one paragraph seemed contradictory to what he said in another. Hence "each proposition is a golden jewel in itself, but has never been combined in a regal diadem of truths." Ripley felt this error was serious since it hindered the attempt to sway others through a clear exposition of ideas. A more serious fault was the passionless tone of his style; for, though a great mind certainly spoke from the pages, the mind seemed one that lacked heart. Because Emerson appeared "stern, frigid, stoical," this flaw, the "cardinal defect," in his writings prevented them from having sufficient moral vigor and vitality.[53]

Thoreau demonstrated the same virtues and faults as Emerson. His style was "true to life," his language was "alive with the deepest spirit of poetry" which penetrated all the beauty and mystery of nature, but he, too, seemed to promote an "ungracious isolation from the living interests of society."[54] He also seemed to advocate a kind of individualism which meant alienation from the rest of mankind, and Ripley greatly feared this attitude since anything that served to drive men farther apart than they already were was dangerous. He worried that the individualism espoused by Emerson and Thoreau could be perverted into justifying irresponsibisity and neglect toward others. Emerson's philosophy of self-reliance could easily be used to buttress the capitalistic theory of a "dog-eat-dog" society.

This distrust of the kind of Transcendentalism that by 1850 was being absorbed into the mainstream of American culture allowed

Ripley to be more sympathetic to those writers who were reacting against Transcendentalism. He gave considerable attention to the writings of Poe, Melville, and Hawthorne; but he concluded that Hawthorne was the best and Poe the worst of the lot. He praised the power of Poe's art "whose uncommon genius it would be folly to deny," but he thought that reading his works was like "breathing the air of a charnel-house. The walls seem to sweat with blood, we stumble on skulls and dead men's hopes, and grinning spectres mock us in the dim, sepulchral light. Even the titles of many of Mr. Poe's tales are nightmares." [55]

Although Poe's genius was undebatable, he lacked the genuineness which called men to the truth of higher laws. It was fine to force readers to plunge into the pit of despair and terror, but Ripley maintained that the artist had to bring them back out again. The experience of evil was a fundamental element of existence, a necessary stage in an individual's growth, but Poe did not complete the initiation cycle. He did not plunge man into darkness and return him to a greater light; he left his reader groping hopelessly in darkness. Hence, since Poe failed to appeal to the universal principles of initiation which demand the glimpse of light at the brink of the pit, his writings therefore "are destitute of truth and naturalness."

Melville and Hawthorne did not fail in this regard. Ripley followed Melville's career from *Typee* (1846) to *Clarel* (1876). He liked *Typee* and *Omoo* for their fresh subject matter and for their vivid pictures. He felt *Mardi* failed, though, because it leaned too heavily on "mystic allegory and this transcendental, glittering, soap-bubble speculation which he has done to death in that ambitious composition." While *Redburn* and *White Jacket* were not altogether free from this excessive discursiveness, they did return to Melville's strength in painting pictures directly from nature. His artistic skill gave the reader the sense that he was actually there, and this reaction was comparable to gazing at the realistic scenes of Dutch paintings and proved that Melville had "the true stuff in him."

Ripley advised Melville to produce more Realistic scenes and to rely upon his eye more than upon his mind. "If he would trust more entirely to the natural play of his imagination without goading it on to a monstrous activity, his work would stand a better chance. . . ." If he confined himself to spinning philosophy out of the stuff of actual experience, his novels would take on the tone of greater genuineness. When philosophy is imposed upon the story instead of grown organically and naturally from it, the effect seems forced and hollow. Melville should therefore excise all those passages of "moral and metaphysical reflections he sets forth in bad Carlylese," for they are only encumbrances to the narrative and interrupt the reader's willing suspension of disbelief. When his novels become essays, they force the reader to become analytic; and the reader ceases to be swayed subtly by the wizard power of art. Melville should, as a novelist, suggest through showing rather than preach by telling.

In *Moby-Dick* Ripley found the fulfillment of his advice. While other critics lamented that the novel lacked the simplicity and adventure of *Typee* and *Omoo,* Ripley lauded *Moby-Dick* as the apex of Melville's artistic genius. Giving it as wide coverage as he could in both *Harper's* and the *Tribune,* he applauded the novel as a "pregnant allegory intended to illustrate the mystery of life. Certain it is that the rapid, pointed hints which are often thrown out with the keenness and velocity of a harpoon penetrate deep into the heart of things, showing that the genius of the author for moral analysis is scarcely surpassed by his wizard power of description." *Moby-Dick* was by far the best production to come from that seething brain "in spite of its lawless flights which put all regular criticism at defiance." The novel was original, perceptive, profound, and so epic in proportion that this "whaliad" would come to be considered a monument of American literature.

As Melville veered from the model of *Moby-Dick* to return to the more abstract allegorical style in *Pierre* and in *The Confidence-Man,* Ripley lost interest in him. He tendered a review of *Clarel* for the purpose of chastising Melville for disregarding those principles that Ripley had spelled out and that Melville had achieved in *Moby-Dick.* Reading this seventeen-thousand-line poem was, to Ripley, like climbing over "a loose mound of sliding stones and gravel in the search for crystals which here and there sparkle from the mass." Not only did Melville revert to his old faults; he became more like Poe in presenting confusion without resolution. The theological doubts and questions he raised in *Clarel* "do not lead to any distinct conclusions"; and in this respect, the work was unlike *Moby-Dick* in which Ishmael progresses from his vision of hell in the Try-Works scene to an experience of paradise in the heartland of the Pacific. Nevertheless, the poem reinforced Ripley's belief that there is a deep "vein of earnestness" in Melville's character and that his "genius had a distinctly poetic side." But he regrets that Melville squandered these qualities by not pursuing the ideal established in *Moby-Dick*.[56]

Although Ripley thought Melville to be a close rival to Hawthorne for the position of America's finest fiction writer, he placed Melville second since Hawthorne's greatness encompassed more than one novel. The points of praise for this man who had once sued the Brook Farm Archon were manifold. Ripley's review of *The Scarlet Letter* was one of the earliest and most favorable. He perceptively noted that Hester worked to capture the reader's imaginative fascination rather than to excite his emotional sympathies. He praised *The Blithedale Romance* for its psychological penetration even though the novel was not so carefully constructed as *The Scarlet Letter,* and he ignored the novel's possible negative reflections on Brook Farm. But the weight of Ripley's admiration for Hawthorne's fiction rested on two major points. In the first place, Hawthorne's genius completed the initiation cycle left truncated by Poe and sometimes by Melville. Although *The Scarlet Letter* certainly had dark and ominous suggestions and ghastly features from which the reader recoiled in horror, the novel also provided "redeeming touches of natural sweetness and beauty which relieve the somber gloom of that work." Hawthorne successfully mixed his lights and darks to portray the complexity of existence, a complexity that went beyond the pure pessimism and bleakness of Poe's pit. Moreover, Ripley valued Hawthorne's "refined comic humor" which was one way of creating light by sweeping away conventional hypocrisies and inflated social pretensions. In this sense, "if Mr. Hawthorne disclaims being the prophet of a noble Future for Humanity, he is an effective pioneer in laying waste the artificial and hollow and deceptive fixtures which now delay its approach." Thus Ripley could readily comprehend why the Transcendentalists respected this man who so often criticized them. In describing life truthfully, realistically, and naturally, he was one of those who cleared away the old forms so that a new, more noble life could be created.

His humor, more sophisticated than mere jokes or puns, was the second main value Ripley found in Hawthorne's work. Far ahead of his time in perceiving this quality, Ripley noted that Hawthorne "opens upon you with the most candid, the most innocent remark — you think the writer one of the most amiable of men, a perfect 'Sunday Child' with no trace of original sin in his nature — but while everything moves softly, swimmingly along, a flash of mischievous pleasantry darts over the page, and you look to see how far the lightning has struck."[57] The effect of this stylistic technique is not only to shake up the reader's established moral principles and philosophical views but to force him to reconsider those values he embraces perhaps too smugly. Such an impact was consummately welcome to Ripley's Transcendental temperament, for only through a revaluation of personal values and an analysis of the self could individual growth and development prosper. Although Hawthorne did not prescribe how a person should grow, he did till the soil which was an essential preliminary step for growth. Again, Ripley viewed Hawthorne as an important participant in the Transcendental movement because he forced a revaluation of principles, even among the Transcendentalists themselves.

In praising Hawthorne for being a "sturdy realist" and his work for its atmosphere of "singular life-like reality," the basis for Ripley's appreciation of the Realist movement of the 1870's is bared. Since he believed that a truthful depiction of life would penetrate to the core of existence and reveal the needs and aspirations of the human heart — needs and goals which in his Transcendental faith Ripley believed to be directed ultimately toward goodness and divinity — he looked upon the new literary movement with enthusiastic sympathy. The public as well took the regionalist writers to heart because, Ripley mused, they longed for a "barbaric yawp" to balance the effeminate fiction of England and the East Coast.

But the public, Ripley cautioned, should exercise discrimination. John Hay ought not to be confused with Joaquin Miller, for the former is a much better writer. Writers like Hay were inspired by a true "sense of the manifold condition of life; they presented faithful pictures of actual human experience"; and their language was fraught with "primeval strength." Sturdy Realists, they qualify as Transcendentalists since ". . . they are true to the supreme instincts of the Ideal, striving to penetrate beneath the crust of conventionalism to the depth of reality, raising the spirit above the letter, while the shams and pretenses of artificial life fall to the ground in 'the middlin' tight grip on the handful of things' about which there is no mistake." Hay's style was admirable in its naturalness. His humor and language came spontaneously, seemingly unbidden, "like oil from the rock."

Miller, on the contrary, offers nothing to raise a man above himself, "to quicken the aspirations of his better nature and reveal a vision of Heaven amid the sorrows and shortcomings of this 'dim diurnal sphere'." If Miller's cynical and misanthropic temperament and the somber gloom of his writings were not enough, his stereotypical characters, his inability to develop climax, the monotone of his pitch, and the other defects like using the word "brown" eighteen times in one poem should suffice to prevent taking him seriously. Writers like John Hay, Edward Eggleston, and Mark Twain, "our inveterate American humorist," were of the first caliber; but men like Petroleum V. Nasby and Joaquin Miller, though the darlings of James R. Lowell, Lincoln, and the Republican party, were lesser literary lights.[58]

Ripley's greatest praise, however, was reserved for the kind of Realism championed by William Dean Howells and Henry James. Although he could not abide Howells' plays, quickly tiring of their "superficial conflicts and feelings," he enjoyed his novels considerably. Even though the subject remained the same — "the unvarnished recital of events that but yesterday took place within the circle of our own experience" — the novel allowed for larger development of this subject than did drama. Because of the novel's greater length, its increase of events and circumstances, and its possibility of point of view, Howells could present a "refined and subtle analysis" of character and the psychological import of events. Howells also excelled in his expressive descriptions, his sense of humor, and his ear for dialect and the natural way people spoke.[59]

Great as Howells was, Ripley believed he was not on the same level as James. In fact, Ripley even used an article devoted nominally to one of Howells' plays to praise James and to explain how James, along with Hawthorne and Emerson, had more influence on American intellectuals. Moreover, Ripley eagerly championed America's greatest novelist and defended him against foreign and domestic critics who, in the London *Atheneum,* charged James with being tedious and who, in the *Tribune,* complained that James lacked humor, that his characters were wooden and flat, and that his novels were "dreary nonentities." Ripley responded by asserting that the fault lay with the reader, not with the writer, for lovers of sensational and melodramatic fiction would, of course, have small appreciation for James. Such readers wanted either the superficiality of the grotesque or the soporific; they desired to grow either wide-eyed with titillation or to read "with one eye closed and the other not open." Although James's art satisfied none of these demands, he was formalistically a genius whose novels were "far removed from the mass of conventional, not to say mechanical, work" with which the markets of England and America were glutted. Stylistically, his language was rich and pure, fluent, and copious; it was "so finely shaded yet capable of such varied service that it is in itself a form of genius."

In addition to genius, James also excelled in genuineness. To Ripley, the reader had such confidence in James's approach to fine psychological problems that the sensitive reader involuntarily shared the belief that the concerns of the characters were actual and important. James accomplished this feat with the tone of a scientist of acute observation, deep insight, and refined analysis who was brooding over the psychical entanglements of his characters: "He delights in the study and representation of personal traits which, though not eccentric, are original and illustrate natural but suggestive qualities of human character. He experiments with the passions as old alchemists did with the metals, not so much with the view of transmuting dross into gold, as of exhibiting accustomed forms in novel and original combinations." As a result, James achieved the frame of mind Ripley called for in his political and philosophical as well as in his esthetic promulgations — that the intellectual pursue a profound and objective analysis of the psychological needs, drives, and motives of human nature. An artistic genius, James had the right philosophical temperament which was a necessary step to an intelligent understanding of the human psyche.

But a danger loomed here, the same danger that Ripley espied in Emerson. In being scientific, objective, and analytical, one ran the risk of being heartless. A highly developed mentality may, as with Hawthorne's Ethan Brand, cause ossification of the heart. Ripley feared this quality in James, for he felt that James was overly distanced from his characters and that his works lacked a "profound and universal human sympathy."[60] Since Ripley believed that the critic should be a guide, not a tyrant, he encouraged James to pursue the beckonings of his own genius, and Ripley would not dictate the means by which the truths of the human heart should be probed. James's genius was unmistakable; his sincerity and seriousness were unquestionable. Ripley believed that was the esthetic maximum the critic could demand of the artist.

Ripley thus performed as a genial and open-minded critic who could appreciate a broad spectrum of writings without being indiscriminate in his praise. His Transcendental background served him well in establishing a useful set of esthetic expectations for fiction. His coeval requirements of genius and genuineness allowed him to make many intelligent evaluations based upon literary criteria, not moral standards nor political dogma. His appraisals are largely sound, and time has seconded most of his judgments.

The two notable exceptions are Whitman and Poe. His low estimate of Whitman is inexcusable. In spite of the reasons he gave, Ripley should have been able to recognize Whitman's greatness. That he did not indicates failure. With Poe, the issue is not as clear. Ripley did not fear terror and gloom, but he felt that Poe's portrayal of unrelenting darkness was not realistic because it did not accurately reflect the complexity, ambiguity, and antithetical lights and darks of life. Moreover, Ripley believed that the revelation of truth spelled the awakening of goodness, a belief that Poe did not share. The twentieth century has chosen to side with Poe, not Ripley, and it is remarkable that so many of Ripley's evaluations hold up given this difference of temperament. Perhaps the lesson to be drawn from this fact is that a literary critic's personal and philosophical beliefs are secondary to the essential requirement that he appraise a given literary work through an intellectually honest method. This important achievement among others must be granted George Ripley.

CHAPTER 6

Conclusion

RIPLEY'S New York years were crowned with many successes: the *Cyclopaedia* made him wealthy; he hobnobbed with all the intellectual giants of the time and formed friendships with many of them; he basked in the public's adulation as the arbiter of taste and intellect for nearly thirty years; and he helped establish the National Institute of Literature, Art, and Science in 1869. Moreover, his personal life was also filled with genteel joy. In 1865 he married Louisa Schlossberger, a vivacious German widow so young that he had first considered adopting her. Together they enjoyed balls, parties, soirées, and became regular members of the social scene. In 1866 Ripley and Louisa visited the land of Kant and Schleiermacher, a trip he had always wanted to make. He toured Europe again in 1869, this time more extensively. The last twenty years of his life were spent in doing the work that he enjoyed and in meeting people who were pleasant and who appreciated his good humor, impressive intellect, and formidable reputation.

Ironically, the material and social successes of his last years have led many critics to see the last phase of his career as a betrayal of the principles of his ministerial and Brook Farm days, but an objective analysis of Ripley's later career refutes this interpretation. His contributions to a wide variety of magazines indicate that his faith remained strong and that his mind pursued the forefront of nearly every political, philosophical, and literary movement of the century. Instead of a decline, his New York years were a continuation, perhaps a culmination, of his growth. His entire adult life can be seen to be all of one piece — to be an organic whole which, like a flower, experienced perpetual growth and perennial blossomings. On Independence Day, 1880, when he was found in his study with his latest thought half written in his lap, no other death would have been as consonant with the life of this man.

Today Ripley is a ghost figure. He appears in many appendices and footnotes, but he is rarely studied as a central figure. In part, this circumstance is due to the fact that he joined no camp: he offends conservatives and frustrates radicals because he fits no tidy political pigeonhole. Partly, this neglect results from Brook Farm; for, since it was his most dramatic experiment, scholars tend to overlook his earlier and his later work. Because the commune was a financial failure, critics tend to slight its objectives, principles, realizations, and accomplishments. His educational and industrial efforts are all but ignored. His five years' work on *The Harbinger,* the main voice of American reform movements of the era, is neglected, as is his program to raise the level of American consciousness through three sets of encyclopaedias.

But the main reason for Ripley's near obscurity is that he is labeled a Transcendentalist, and every Transcendentalist has been considered secondary when compared to that high priest of Transcendentalism — Ralph Waldo Emerson. Transcendentalism, which focuses on those ripe moments of inspiration everyone experiences at one time or another, is the special moment which Abraham Maslow calls a "peak experience" and which Friedrich Nietzsche calls "revelation." In that sense, Transcendentalism means transcending the baggage of life — progressing from an ignorant existence to a sapient state. Such an achievement does not mean the Oriental transcendence of reality that is mystical but pragmatic American Transcendentalism.

Within this context of American Transcendentalism, Ripley is distinct from Emerson who often believed that a saturnalia of the mind was sufficient and did not worry about whether this psychologically exhilarating experience would be magnanimous. As Emerson says in "Self-Reliance," truthfulness of self-knowledge is more important than goodness. "If I am the Devil's child," Emerson confesses, "I will live then from the Devil." Such thoughts were anathema to Ripley and were the basis of his distrust of Emerson, Thoreau, and Whitman. His primary quest as a Transcendentalist was to find a means to make individualism spiritually significant and socially beneficial, to reconcile the age-old problem of self-love and brotherly love. He did not believe that evil was a counterpart of good but a palpable foe to be fought valiantly and unrelentingly. He did not believe that man was basically good but, like Hawthorne's Pearl, a creature endowed with a magnificent capacity for good or for evil.

Hence, Ripley could not agree with Emerson that "a man is counterpoise to the city." Instead, he believed in environmental conditioning and felt responsible for investigating means by which man's environment could be structured to cultivate his angelic qualities while letting his diabolical tendencies wither. While Ripley might at times equal Thoreau's diatribes against materialism, he knew that "Simplicity, simplicity, simplicity" was a futile appeal and that the main problem was to regulate the power of social structures, not to hide from it. Perhaps lacking Emerson's genius, he sought to regulate such genius by insisting that personal insight must be checked by the experience of a community of souls, that personal inspiration must be authenticated by the revelations of others. Otherwise, individualism might merely spell idiosyncrasy, might drive Jones Very insane, frustrate Orestes Brownson into fideism, excuse some for social irresponsibility, and encourage others to become smugly arrogant.

Emerson's major complaint against Thoreau was that he failed to engineer for all America. Ripley, who could make that same criticism of Emerson, Whitman, and Thoreau, was not merely a dreamer; he was a dreamer-doer, an idealist with a program, an intellectual with strong hands; for Ripley dared engineer for all America. The possibility of failure did not deter him; financial ruin and social scorn did not discourage him. At the same time, he was as fantastic a dreamer as any of the Emersonian trinity. Emerson might revel in the perpetual "quiz of life," Thoreau might find heaven in a pond, Whitman might find boisterous fulfillment traveling the open road with no destination in mind, but Ripley envisioned a Golden Age where man no longer would be restricted to dreams but would find their realization in life, a New Eden where the gap between reality and idealism would be bridged. He found support for this vision in literature, in the theological views of Jonathan Edwards and Friedrich Schleiermacher, in the political concepts of Charles Fourier and Karl Marx, in the scientific theories of Charles Darwin and Herbert Spencer, and in the common agricultural miracle of a seed struggling to flower in the sun.

Society often tires of such dreamers, but something in man's nature renders such dreamers perennial. Ripley was among the most daring of dreamers. For him, Transcendentalism was a viable and fulfilling life-style, one that did not result in insanity or in fideism or in mere intellectual pastime. Rather, Ripley's Transcendentalism allowed him to experience the challenge of life in wisdom, in faith, and in joy.

Notes and References

Abbreviations used: BPL — Boston Public Library
MHS — Massachusetts Historical Society

Chapter One

1. Ripley letter to George Bancroft, September 20, 1837, Massachusetts Historical Society. In the same letter he praises William Penn's "holy experiment" which emphasized "moulding our institutions after the loftiest idea."
2. See Charles Crowe, *George Ripley* (Athens, Georgia: 1967), pp. 3-14 for a detailed description of Jerome's religion.
3. O. B. Frothingham, *George Ripley* (Boston, 1882), pp. 5-6.
4. Ralph Waldo Emerson, *Emerson's Complete Works* (Cambridge, 1890), X, 362.
5. Frothingham, pp. 7-8.
6. Crowe, p. 26. Thomas W. Dorr, who later became famous for leading a similar uprising in Rhode Island, was one of the conciliators in this rebellion.
7. Frothingham, pp. 10-11.
8. Ripley, *Commonplace Book,* entry #36, Houghton Library.
9. Ibid., entry #49.
10. Ibid., November, 1822.
11. Frothingham, p. 22.
12. Ibid., p. 23.
13. Ripley letter to his sister, Elizabeth G. Brigham, in the possession of Charles Brigham as quoted in the unpublished dissertation (Wisconsin, 1941) by Howard K. Wilson, "George Ripley, Social and Literary Critic," p. 34. Another theory is possible: Ripley may have wished to attend Harvard all along and used negative psychology on Jerome.
14. Ibid., p. 34.
15. Frothingham, p. 24.
16. Ibid., pp. 30-31.
17. Ripley, "Edward A. Park's *Life of Professor B. B. Edwards,*" review clipping, Houghton Library.

Chapter Two

1. Frothingham, p. 39.

2. Ripley manuscript, "Improvement Constitution," Massachusetts Historical Society. Ripley letter to George C. Shattuck, September 29, 1831, Massachusetts Historical Society. Ripley letter to Longfellow, September 2, 1834, Houghton Library. In a letter from Samuel May to Henry Chapman, November 10, 1840, May places Ripley's name at the head of a list of prospective Bostonian speakers on antislavery, Boston Public Library.

3. Ripley, "Letter to a Trinitarian Friend," *Tracts of the American Unitarian Association* (Boston, 1833), VI, 193-204. Ripley, "The Divinity of Jesus Christ," *Tracts* (1830,1831), III, 213-40.

4. Ripley, "Letter to Purchase Street Church," October 1, 1840, MHS.

5. Ripley, *Commonplace Book,* February 4, 1827, Houghton Library.

6. Ibid., c. 1829-30.

7. See Norman Ware, *The Industrial Worker: 1840-60* (Chicago, 1964). Arthur Kinoy's "Arise and Depart, For This Is Not Your Rest" analyzes the factors leading to Ripley's resignation (Bowdoin Prize, Harvard, April 1, 1941).

8. Frothingham, p. 74.

9. Ripley letter to J. S. Dwight, July 7, 1840, Boston Public Library.

10. Ripley, "Letter to Purchase Street Church," MHS.

11. Sydney B. Ahlstrom, *Transcendentalism in New England* (Boston, 1930), p. 8.

12. R. C. Albrecht, *Theodore Parker* (New York, 1971), p. 42. Parker showed his sermon to Ripley who agreed that it was weak and repetitive.

13. Ripley, "Religion in France," *Christian Examiner,* X (July, 1831), 277.

14. Ripley, "De Gérando on Self-Education," *Christian Examiner,* IX (September, 1830), 71.

15. Ripley, "Herder's Theological Opinions," *Christian Examiner,* XIX (November, 1835), 180.

16. "De Gérando," p. 74.

17. Ripley, "Theological Aphorisms," *Christian Examiner,* XXI (January, 1837), 385-98.

18. Ripley, "Martineau's *Rationale,*" *Christian Examiner,* XXI (November, 1836), 245.

19. Ibid., p. 254.

20. Ibid., p. 247.

21. Ibid., p. 227.

22. Ripley, "A Public Letter Written in Reply to Andrews Norton," *Boston Daily Advertiser,* XLII, November 9, 1836. Reprinted in part in Perry Miller, *The Transcendentalists* (Cambridge, 1950), pp. 162-63.

23. Orville Dewey, "The Dudleian Lecture," *Christian Examiner,* XXI, September, 1826. See Miller, p. 158.

24. C. H. Faust, "The Background of the Unitarian Opposition to Transcendentalism," *Modern Philology,* XXXV (February, 1938), 300-1.

25. In 1830 F. W. P. Greenwood of Harvard praised the liberality of the Cambridge Divinity School and claimed that Unitarianism was not committed to "a timid creed-bound theology" and complained that Calvinism's "*exclusiveness is its utter* diversion." In a tract for the American Unitarian Association, James Walker reiterated these sentiments. Faust, pp. 322-24.

26. Ripley, Preface to *Discourses on the Philosophy of Religion* (Boston, 1836). All quotations from the *Discourses* are from this eighty-page text.

27. René Dubos adopts a similar attitude in his latest book, *The God Within* (New York, 1972).

28. As quoted in John Weiss, *Discourses Occasioned by the Death of Convers Francis* (Cambridge, 1863), p. 28. Brownson as quoted in Jeter Isely, "A Note on George Ripley," *Unitarian Historical Society Proceedings,* XIII (1961), 85. Alexander Kern, "The Rise of Transcendentalism," *Transitions in American Literary History* (Durham, 1953), p. 256. Sidney E. Ahlstrom, Review of Charles Crowe's *George Ripley* in *American Literature,* XL (November, 1968), 404.

29. Ripley, "Theological Aphorisms," and Bowen, "Emerson's *Nature,*" *Christian Examiner,* XXI (January, 1837), 385-98 and 371-85. Ripley's *Discourses* were mentioned on page 403 of this issue as a book which "may be confidently referred to as one of the happiest among the many indications we have had of late, of a disposition to introduce a higher tone of spirituality into the preaching of Unitarians."

30. Joseph Slater, "George Ripley and Thomas Carlyle," *Publications of the Modern Language Association,* LXVII (June, 1952), 341. Ms. in Pierpont Morgan Library, New York.

31. Ripley letter to Carlyle, December 29, 1836, Houghton Library.

32. Ripley, "Carlyle's *Life of Sterling,*" *Tribune,* November 8, 1851.

33. See article on Carlyle in *New American Cyclopaedia* (New York, 1858). Ripley, "The Carlyle Anthology," *Tribune,* November 14, 1876.

34. See Joel Myerson, "A Calendar of Transcendental Club Meetings," *American Literature,* XLIV (May, 1972), 197-207.

35. Isely, "Note on Ripley," p. 84.

36. Miller, *Transcendentalists,* p. 213.

37. Albrecht, *Parker,* p. 34.

38. Miller, p. 227.

39. Ripley, *"The Latest Form of Infidelity" Examined* (Boston, 1839), p. 42.

40. Ibid., p. 114.

41. Ripley, *Philosophical Miscellanies* (Boston, 1838), I, 35-36.

42. Ripley letter to Convers Francis, January 17, 1837, Boston Public Library.

43. Ripley letter to Longfellow, March 2, 1837, Houghton Library.
44. René Welleck, "The Minor Transcendentalists and German Philosophy," *New England Quarterly,* XV (1942), 652.
45. Ripley, "Cousin's *Course of the History of Modern Philosophy,*" *Tribune* clipping, Houghton Library.
46. Ripley, *Specimens of Foreign Standard Literature* (Boston, 1838), I, 37. Ripley includes Jouffroy, Reid, and Dugald Stewart in the school of Eclecticism.
47. Woodbridge I. Riley, *American Thought* (Gloucester, 1915), p. 395.
48. Ripley letter to J. F. Clarke, December, 8, 1840, Houghton Library.
49. "The Art of Life," *Dial,* I (October, 1840), 175-82. While Ripley is probably the author of this article as Clarence Gohdes argues, the matter is not yet settled.
50. Ripley letter to J. S. Dwight, August 6, 1840, Boston Public Library. Since this letter is from Brook Farm, Ripley must have written "1840" for "1841."
51. Ripley letter to Emerson, October? 1840?, Houghton Library.
52. Ripley letter to J. F. Clarke, March 15, 1837, Houghton Library.
53. Ripley letter to Dwight, August 14, 1838, Massachusetts Historical Society.
54. Ripley, "Farewell Discourse," March 8, 1841, MHS.
55. Ripley, "The Claims of the Age on the Work of the Evangelist," May 20, 1840, MHS. The sermon influenced Dwight so that a fast race was run between the sermon's publication and Dwight's expulsion from the pulpit.
56. Ripley, "On Common Sense in the Affairs of Religion," July, 1837, MHS.
57. Caroline H. Dall, *Margaret and Her Friends* (Boston, 1897), pp. 9, 54.

Chapter Three

1. Charles Crowe (*Ripley,* p. 137) says Ripley introduced the plan at an October, 1840, meeting of the Club; but the Club's last official meeting was held on September 20, 1840.
2. Parker, "Poverty" in Albrecht, *Parker,* p. 75. Brownson, "The Laboring Classes," *Selected Writings of the American Transcendentalists* (New York, 1966), p. 267.
3. Emerson, "Chardon Street Convention," *Works,* pp. 352-54.
4. Ripley letter to Emerson, November 9, 1840, Houghton Library.
5. Ripley, *Commonplace Book,* undated but after September 1, 1827, and before March 2, 1830.
6. Caroline Dall, *Transcendentalism in New England* (Boston, 1897), p. 27. Henry Adams, "Transcendentalism in New England," *North American Review,* CXXIII (1876), 471-72.

7. William Ellery Channing letter to Adin Ballou, February 27, 1841, as quoted in Frothingham, p. 115.
8. Margaret Fuller letter to Emerson, May 31, 1840, Boston Public Library.
9. Richard Chamber, ed., *The Book of Days* (Philadelphia, 1893).
10. Ripley letter to Emerson, November 9, 1840, Houghton Library.
11. Crowe, *Ripley,* p. 129.
12. John Van Der Zee Sears, *My Friends at Brook Farm* (New York, 1912), pp. 141-42. John Codman, *Brook Farm* (Boston, 1894), pp. 64, 177-78.
13. Elizabeth Peabody, "Plan of the West Roxbury Community," *Dial,* (January, 1842).
14. Ripley letter to Adin Ballou, September 11, 1844, Boston Public Library.
15. Frothingham, *Ripley,* pp. 147-48.
16. Ibid., pp. 143-44.
17. Ibid., p. 127.
18. Richard Henry Dana, Jr., *An Autobiographical Sketch* (Hamden, Connecticut: 1953), p. 39.
19. Sears, *My Friends,* pp. 108-10.
20. Edmund Quincy letter to Mrs. Henry G. Chapman, August 2, 1844, Boston Public Library.
21. Crowe, *Ripley,* p. 144.
22. Sears, *My Friends,* p. 162.
23. Ripley letter to Emerson, December 17, 1841, Houghton Library.
24. Ripley letter to Richard H. Dana, Sr., December 8, 1845, MHS.
25. Hawthorne letter to David Mack, July 18, 1841, BPL.
26. A. W. Weston to Henry and Maria Chapman, May 18, 1841, BPL.
27. Codman, *Brook Farm,* p. 76.
28. Georgiana Kirby, *Years of Experience* (New York, 1971), p. 89.
29. Marianne Dwight, *Letters from Brook Farm, 1844-7* (Poughkeepsie, 1928), p. 41.
30. Codman, *Brook Farm,* p. 160. An amusing account of how Ripley good-naturedly persuaded people to attend meetings is on page 175.
31. Nora Schetter Blair letter to Ripley, March 5, 1880, MHS.

Chapter Four

1. Sears, *My Friends,* p. 154.
2. Frothingham, p. 158.
3. Ripley letter to Minot Pratt, July 22, 1843, Fruitlands Museum.
4. Maria W. Chapman letter to William Lloyd Garrison, Fall, 1843, BPL. The *Omnibus* is the periodical in question.
5. Samuel Osgood letter to John S. Dwight, November 21, 1840, as quoted in Henry W. Sams, *Autobiography of Brook Farm* (Englewood

Cliffs, 1958), p. 9. Marianne Dwight, *Letters,* p. 171.

6. As quoted in James H. Wilson, *The Life of Charles A. Dana* (New York, 1907), p. 41.

7. Sams, *Autobiography,* pp. 109-10.

8. See Frothingham, pp. 157-64.

9. The North American Phalanx began with eighty people and $8,000, building its capital to $80,000 in nine years before being destroyed by fire. The Wisconsin Phalanx sold its property for 108% of the investments. See Mark Holloway, *Heavens on Earth* (New York, 1966), pp. 135-50.

10. Sams, *Autobiography,* p. 97.

11. Ripley, "What Do You Propose?" *Harbinger,* I (June-December, 1845), 48.

12. John Orvis to Mary L. Tavas, March 15, 1846, MHS. Sams, pp. 144-46.

13. Sams, p. 73.

14. Ibid., p. 154.

15. Friedrich Engels, "Socialism: Utopian and Scientific," *The Essential Left* (New York, 1968), p. 110.

16. These lesser-known Utopian novels are appended to the back of Codman's *Brook Farm,* attesting to the close connection between the renewed interest in Brook Farm and Utopian literature in the 1890's. Arno Press offers new editions of over forty Utopian novels, twenty-eight of which were first published in the late nineteenth century.

17. Ripley, "What Shall We Do?" *Harbinger,* III (December 5, 1846), 411.

18. Frank L. Mott, *A History of American Magazines* (Cambridge, 1957), I, 764.

19. Ripley, "What Shall We Do?" *Harbinger,* III (December 5, 1846). 410.

20. Ripley, "Our Present Attempt" *Harbinger,* II (December 20, 1845), 30; "Forms of Guarantyism," *Harbinger,* III (October 31, 1846), 335.

21. Ripley letter to John S. Dwight, December 7, 1847, and November 22, 1847, BPL.

22. Ripley, "Signs of Progress," *Harbinger,* I (June 28, 1845), 45-47.

23. Ripley, "Close of Our First Volume," *Harbinger,* I (December 6, 1845), 414.

24. Ripley, "Influence of Association on Women," *Harbinger,* III (September 26, 1846), 252; "Anti-Slavery at Washington," *Harbinger,* IV (December 12, 1846), 16.

25. Ripley, "Signs of Progress," *Harbinger,* I (June 28, 1845), 111; "Unitarianism and Association," *Harbinger,* V (October 2, 1847), 270.

26. Ripley, "Signs of the Times," *Harbinger,* III (November 21, 1846), 383; "Our Present Attempt," *Harbinger,* II (December 20, 1845), 30.

27. Ripley, "Notice of Clay's *True American,*" *Harbinger,* I (July 19, 1845), 110.

28. Ripley, "Introductory Notice," *Harbinger,* I (June 14, 1845), 14.
29. Ripley, "Our Present Attempt," *Harbinger,* II (December 20, 1845), 32.
30. Ripley, "Influence of Social Circumstances," *Harbinger,* V (June 26, 1847), 46.
31. Ripley, "Introductory Notices," *Harbinger,* I (June 14, 1845), 16, 8.
32. Ripley, "We Cannot Breathe This Atmosphere," *Harbinger,* III (November 7, 1846), 352.
33. Ripley, "Unitarianism and Association," *Harbinger,* V (October 2, 1847), 269.
34. Ripley letter to John S. Dwight, October 27, 1847, and November 8, 1847, BPL.
35. Ripley letter to John S. Dwight, July 14, 1848, BPL.
36. Ripley letter to John S. Dwight, April 6, 1849, BPL.
37. Ripley letter to John S. Dwight, April 10, 1849, Fruitlands Museum.
38. Ripley letters to John S. Dwight, April 6, 1849, BPL and April 10, 1849, Fruitlands Museum.
39. Ripley letter to Henry W. Bellows, April 17, 1849, MHS. Ripley letter to Theodore Parker, July 27 and May 1, 1849, MHS.
40. Ripley letter to John S. Dwight, April 10, 1849, MHS.
41. Arthur R. Schultz and Henry A. Pochmann, "George Ripley," *American Literature,* XIV (March, 1942), 1-19. Charles Crowe, "Genesis of a Reformer," *Manuscripts,* XI (Spring, 1959), 38.
42. Ripley letter to Parker, September 26, 1853, MHS.
43. Ripley letter to Parker, February 28, 1856, MHS.
44. Samuel E. Morison, *The Oxford History of the American People* (New York, 1965), p. 574. Hawthorne, preface to *The Marble Faun* (Boston, 1860).

Chapter Five

1. Ripley letter to Theodore Parker, July 31, 1852, MHS.
2. Crowe, *Ripley,* pp. 240, vii.
3. Samuel A. Eliot, *Heralds of a Liberal Faith* (Boston, 1910), pp. 330-35.
4. Ripley letter to Reverend Edward Abbot, February 28, 1874, Houghton Library. Ripley letter to R. H. Dana, Jr., February 12, 1858, MHS.
5. Ripley, "*Works of Shakespeare* by H. N. Hudson," *Tribune,* February 2, 1852.
6. Crowe, *Ripley,* p. 240.
7. Henry M. Christman and Charles Blitzer, *The American Journalism of Marx and Engels* (New York, 1966), p. xviii.
8. Ripley letter to John S. Dwight, September 6, 1849, BPL.

9. Ripley, *Tribune* clipping, 1852, Houghton Library.

10. Ripley, "Moses Stuart," *Tribune,* June 5, 1850; "Richard Hildreth," *Tribune,* February 18, 1851.

11. "Henry Stanton's *Sketches of Reforms and Reformers,*" *Tribune,* December 1, 1849. "Barrow's *L'avengro,*" *Tribune,* March 14, 1851.

12. "Bristed's Letter to Horace Mann," *Tribune,* June 4, 1850. "Peabody's Polish-American System," *Tribune,* September 14, 1850.

13. "Literature and the Labor Question," *Tribune,* March 26, 1851.

14. "Beecher's *True Remedy for the Wrongs of Women,*" *Tribune,* August 26, 1851. "Oakes' *Woman and Her Needs,*" *Tribune,* October 31, 1851.

15. "Elliott's *New-England History,*" *Tribune,* April 4, 1857.

16. "De Gurowski's *America and Europe*," *Tribune*, April 25, 1857.

17. "Bancroft's *History of the United States,*" *Tribune,* March 20, 1852. Frothingham, pp. 208-09. Charles Sumner letter to Ripley, July 5, 1849, MHS. Ripley letter to Theodore Parker, October 5, 1856, MHS.

18. Ripley letter to Charlotte Dana, October 7, 1861, MHS. Crowe gives a detailed account of Sophia's death, *Ripley,* pp. 236-7.

19. "Frothingham's 'The Morality of the Riot'," *Tribune,* July 30, 1863. "Headley's *The Great Rebellion,*" *Tribune,* February 4, 1863.

20. Ripley letter to J. T. Fisher, December 27, 1852, MHS. "John Fiske," *Tribune,* August 25, 1869.

21. "The Death of George Ripley," *The Socialist,* IV (1880), 311.

22. "Stephen Andrews' *The Science of Society,*" *Tribune,* January 24, 1851. "Lamartine's *England in 1850,*" *Tribune,* June 27, 1851.

23. "The International Review," *Tribune,* November 5, 1878.

24. "Henry Ammon James' *Communism in America,*" *Tribune,* May 13, 1879. "Literature and the Labor Question," *Tribune,* March 26, 1851. "Homes of American Authors," *Tribune* clipping, undated, Houghton Library.

25. "In Memory of Mazzini," *Tribune,* May 30, 1878. There were two hundred declared Communists in America led by Justus Schwab and Henry Drury. "The Present State of Russia," *Tribune* clipping, undated, Houghton Library.

26. Ripley letter to Parker, July 31, 1852, MHS.

27. "Cousin's *History of Modern Philosophy,*" *Tribune,* April 24, 1852.

28. Ripley letter to George Bancroft, August 11, 1863, MHS. "Cook on Biology," *Tribune,* October 26, 1877. "Humboldt's Cosmos," *Tribune,* July 24, 1851. "Huxley's Evidence as to Man's Place in Nature," *Tribune,* July 6, 1863. "Spencer's *Data of Ethics,*" *Tribune,* July 18, 1859. "Spencer's *Science of Society,*" *Tribune,* April 27, 1875.

29. "Coues' *System of Mechanical Philosophy,*" *Tribune,* May 10, 1851.

30. "Rochester Rappings," *Tribune,* November 29, 1849. "An Evening with the Spirits," *Tribune,* June 8, 1850. "More About the Spirits," *Tribune,* June 21, 1850. "The Philosophy of Spiritual Intercourse," *Tribune,* March 22, 1851.

31. "Swedenborg and Channing," *Tribune,* November 5, 1878. "James' *Substance and Shadow,*" *Tribune,* August 7, 1863.

32. "E. A. Washburn's *The Issue of Modern Philosophy,*" *Tribune,* December 13, 1850.

33. Ripley letter to Bancroft, March 15, 1878, MHS.

34. "Comte's *Systeme de Politique Positive,*" *Tribune,* May 22, 1852. "The Positive Philosophy of Comte," *Tribune* clipping, Houghton Library.

35. Ripley letter to Bancroft, March? 1878?, MHS.

36. Ripley, Working notes on Bascom, 1878? MHS. Notes on the "Eternal World," January 15, 1878, MHS.

37. Ripley, notes on Hartmann's *Philosophie due Unbewussten,* November, 1877, MHS. Notes on "Personal Experience," November, 1877, MHS.

38. "Death of Sainte-Beuve," *Tribune,* November 5, 1869.

39. "William Morris' *Jason,*" *Harper's,* XXXVI (December, 1867), 125-26. "Tennyson's *Queen Mary,*" *Tribune,* July 2, 1875.

40. "Ouida's *Under Two Flags,*" *Tribune,* October 17, 1867. "Queechy," *Tribune* clipping, Houghton Library.

41. "Dickens' *Little Dorrit,*" *Tribune,* June 23, 1857. "Dickens' *Hard Times,*" *Tribune* clipping, Houghton Library.

42. "Thackeray's *Roundabout Papers,*" *Tribune,* November 28, 1863. "Arthur Pendennis," *Harper's,* II (February, 1851), 428. "Henry Esmond," *Tribune* clipping, Houghton Library. "Thackeray's Early and Late Papers," *Tribune,* June 6, 1867.

43. "William Mayo's *The Berber,*" *Tribune,* November 13, 1850.

44. "Eliot's *Romola,*" *Harper's,* XXVII (September, 1863), 562. *"Middlemarch,"* *Tribune,* January 3, 1873. "Memoirs of George Sand," *Putnam's,* IX (February, June, 1857), 175-87 and 598-613. Frank L. Mott considers this last to be the best contemporary article on Sand, *History,* II, 163.

45. "The Issue of Modern Philosophical Thought," *Tribune,* December 13, 1850.

46. "St. Leger: Or, the Threads of Love," *Tribune,* December 25, 1849. "Poems by Alexander Smith," *Tribune* clipping, Houghton Library. "Reply to Dr. Korner," *Tribune,* February 27, 1851.

47. *"The Courtship of Miles Standish,"* *Tribune,* October 12, 1858. "Longfellow's *The Sea-Side and the Fire Side,*" *Tribune,* January 1, 1850. "Holmes' *Astraema,*" *Tribune,* October 16, 1850. "Duyckinck's *Cyclopaedia,*" *Putnam's,* VII (February, 1856), 170-73.

48. "Whittier's *The Chapel of the Hermits,*" *Tribune,* February 4, 1853. *"The Tent on the Beach," Tribune,* March 21, 1867. *"The Poetical Works of Whittier," Tribune,* June 22, 1857. "Meissner's *The Last Years of Heine,*" *Putnam's,* VIII (November, 1856), 517-26.

49. Ripley letter to Henry T. Tuckerman, June 27, 1861, Houghton Library.

50. "Notes on Walt Whitman," *Tribune,* June 20, 1867.

51. "Edwin Arnold's *Light of Asia,*" *Tribune,* October 12, 1879.

52. Ripley letter to Parker, February 28, 1856 and March 9, 1858, MHS.

53. *"Representative Men," Tribune,* January 22, 1850. "May Day and Other Pieces," *Tribune,* May 2, 1867. "Emerson's Perpetual Forces," *Tribune,* September 4, 1877.

54. "Thoreau's *Excursions,*" *Tribune,* October 31, 1863.

55. *"The Works of E. A. Poe," Tribune,* January 19, 1850.

56. *"Redburn," Tribune,* December 1, 1849. *"White Jacket," Tribune,* April 5, 1850. *"Moby-Dick," Harper's,* IV (December, 1851), 137. *"Moby-Dick," Tribune,* November 22, 1851. "Melville's *Clarel,*" *Tribune,* June 16, 1876.

57. *"House of the Seven Gables," Tribune,* April 26, 1851. "Alice Carey's *Hagar,*" *Tribune* clipping, Houghton Library. *"Our Old Home," Tribune,* October 3, 1863. "Hawthorne's *House,*" *Harper's,* II (May, 1851), 855-56. See also "Hawthorne's *Letter,*" *Tribune,* November 9, 1877. *"Blithedale Romance," Tribune,* July 22, 1852. *"Twice-Told Tales," Tribune,* March 22, 1851. *"The Snow-Image," Tribune,* January 18, 1851.

58. "Hay's *Pike County Ballads,*" *Tribune,* May 31, 1871. "Miller's *Songs of the Sierras,*" *Tribune,* September 29, 1871. "Eggleston's *Circuit-Rider,*" *Tribune,* April 17, 1874. *"The Hoosier Schoolmaster," Tribune,* February 27, 1872. *"Roughing It," Tribune,* January 31, 1873. "Nasby's *Swingin' Round the Cirkle," Tribune,* January 26, 1867.

59. "Howells' *Out of the Question,*" *Tribune,* May 4, 1877. *"The Lady of the Aroostook," Tribune,* March 11, 1879. See also *"A Counterfeit Presentiment," Tribune,* October 19, 1877 and *"Italian Journeys," Tribune,* December 5, 1867.

60. "Mr. James and His New Story, *Washington Square,*" *Tribune,* June 13, 1880. "Mr. James and His Reviewers: *The Europeans,*" *Tribune,* November 2, 1878. "James' *Confidence,*" *Tribune,* March 5, 1880. "James' *Hawthorne,*" *Tribune,* February 3, 1880. "James' *The American,*" *Tribune,* May 8, 1877.

Selected Bibliography

Since a comprehensive list of Ripley's writings is virtually impossible, what follows is a highly selective bibliography. The thousands of articles he wrote for over a dozen magazines, newspapers, and periodicals have not yet been bibliographed, and it would take a book in itself to do so. The 424 letters of his known to exist are in thirteen places and are uncatalogued. The entries for Ripley in *American Literary Manuscripts* (Austin, 1960) are untrustworthy. The bibliography in Charles Crowe's biography is more complete but is still only exploratory.

PRIMARY SOURCES

1. Books (in order of publication):

Discourses on the Philosophy of Religion Addressed to Doubters Who Wish to Believe. Boston: James Munroe, November 18, 1836.

The Temptations of the Times. Boston: Hilliard, Gray, 1837.

Philosophical Miscellanies. Boston: Hilliard, Gray, 1838.

Specimens of Foreign Standard Literature. Edited by George Ripley. 14 vols. Boston: Hilliard, Gray, 1838-1842.

"The Latest Form of Infidelity" Examined: A Letter to Mr. Andrews Norton of Cambridge Divinity School by an Alumnus of that School. Boston: James Munroe, September 5, 1839.

A Handbook of Literature and the Fine Arts. Edited by Ripley and Bayard Taylor. New York: A. S. Barnes, 1852.

The New American Cyclopaedia. Edited by Ripley and Charles A. Dana. 16 vols. New York, London: Appleton, 1862, 1884.

Books and Men: A Series of Critical and Biographical Sketches. Unpublished ms. Preface to projected anthology of Ripley's writings. Boston. Massachusetts Historical Society, O. B. Frothingham box, July 8, 1862.

2. Sermons and Tracts:

"The Claims of the Age on the Work of the Evangelist: A sermon preached at the ordination of John Sullivan Dwight." Boston. Massachusetts Historical Society, Frothingham box, May 20, 1840.

"The Divinity of Jesus Christ." *Tracts of the American Unitarian Association,* III. Boston: Gray and Bowen, 1830, 1831, 213-40.

"A Letter to a Trinitarian Friend." *Tracts of the American Unitarian Association,* VI. Boston: Charles Bowen, March, 1833, 193-204.

"A Farewell Discourse." Boston. Massachusetts Historical Society, Ms. March 8, 1841.
"Jesus Christ, the Same, Yesterday, Today, and Forever: A sermon preached at the installation of Orestes Brownson." Boston. Massachusetts Historical Society, Ms. May 14, 1834.
"A Letter Addressed to the Congregational Church in Purchase Street." Boston. Massachusetts Historical Society, Ms. October 1, 1840.
"On Common Sense in the Affairs of Religion." Boston. Massachusetts Historical Society, Ms. July, 1837.

3. Essays and Articles (see notes to Chapter Five for writings after 1850):
A. *The Christian Examiner*
"De Gérando on Self-Education," IX (September, 1830), 70-107.
"Religion in France," X (July, 1831), 273-96.
"Pestalozzi," XI (January, 1832), 347-73.
"Mackintosh's *Ethical Philosophy*," XIII (January, 1833), 311-32.
"Professor Marsh's Translation of Herder," XVIII (May, 1835), 167-221.
"Herder's Theological Opinions and Services," XIX (November, 1835), 172-204.
"Martineau's *Rationale*," XXI (November, 1836), 225-54.
"Theological Aphorisms," XXI (January, 1837), 385-98.
B. *The Dial*
"Brownson's Writings," I (1840), 22-46.
"Letter to a Theological Student," I (1840), 183-7.
C. *The Harbinger*
"Introductory Notice," I (June 14, 1845), 8-10.
"Influence of Machinery," I (June 14, 1845), 14.
"Tendencies of Modern Civilization," I (June 28, 1845), 33-35.
"Andrew Jackson," I (June 28, 1845), 45-47.
"Influence of Social Circumstances," V (June 26, 1847), 46.

4. Manuscripts:
Boston Public Library. Thirty-seven letters in the Dwight Collection; thirty-five in the Brook Farm collection; eighteen in the Antislavery Collection; seventeen in the Weston Papers. 1836-1870.
Fruitlands Museum. Ten letters. 1841-1847.
Houghton Library, Harvard University. Commonplace Book (MS Am 860), clippings (fMS Am 931.1), Brook Farm account book (fMS Am 931), fifteen letters collected in four Ripley folders (fMS Am 931.1).
Massachusetts Historical Society. Memorandum book, sermons, manuscripts and thirty-four letters in the Frothingham collection, thirty-eight letters in the Bancroft Collection, eighteen in the Parker papers, seventeen in the Dana Collection. 1830-1880.

New York *Herald Tribune* Files. 106 letters, notes and memoranda, 1849-1880.

5. Anthologies (which offer a sampling of Ripley's writings):

HOCHFIELD, GEORGE, ed. *Selected Writings of the American Transcendentalists.* New York: New American Library, 1966.

MILLER, PERRY, ed. *The Transcendentalists.* Cambridge: Harvard University Press, 1950.

SAMS, HENRY W., ed. *Autobiography of Brook Farm.* Englewood Cliffs: Prentice-Hall, 1958.

SECONDARY SOURCES

ADAMS, HENRY. "Transcendentalism in New England." *North American Review,* CXXIII (1876), 468-74. An opponent of Transcendentalism calls Brook Farm "the lawful outcome of Transcendentalism."

ALCOTT, A. BRONSON. *Concord Days.* Boston: Roberts Brothers, 1872. Gives an account of Brook Farm, Fruitlands, and Ripley's influence on the Concord circle.

BOLLER, PAUL F. *American Transcendentalism, 1830-1860.* New York: Putnam's, 1974. Ripley is mentioned over thirty times in this overview of the movement.

BOWEN, FRANCIS. "Emerson's *Nature.*" *Christian Examiner,* XXI (January, 1837), 371-85. First intelligent published attack on Ripley, Emerson, *et al.*

BROOKS, VAN WYCK. *The Flowering of New England.* New York: Dutton, 1936. Discusses Ripley briefly as one member of this pre-Civil War movement.

BROWNSON, ORESTES. *"Brook Farm." Democratic Review* (November, 1842), 481-96. Detailed analysis of possible reform movements; concludes that Ripley's plan is the best.

BUELL, LAWRENCE. *Literary Transcendentalism.* Ithaca: Cornell University Press, 1973. Links Ripley's esthetic principles with the general esthetic principles of the Transcendentalists.

CODMAN, JOHN T. *Brook Farm.* Boston: Arena, 1894. Personal reminiscence by a former Brook Farm student.

COOKE, GEORGE WILLIS. *An Introduction to the Dial.* 2 vols. Cleveland: Rowfont, 1902. Praises Ripley for being "one of the earliest and most consistent of the Transcendentalists."

———. "George Ripley," in *Heralds of a Liberal Faith: The Preachers.* Boston: American Unitarian Association, 1910. Claims Ripley's "critical ability and scholarly insight" were unsurpassed.

CORTISSOZ, ROYAL. *The New York Tribune: Incidents and Personalities in Its History.* New York: New York *Tribune*, 1923. Ripley's colleagues on the *Tribune* admitted his high standards and scholarship but thought him too amiable.

CROWE, CHARLES. "Genesis of a Reformer." *Manuscripts*, XI (Spring, 1959), 1-13, 38. Claims Ripley suffered bitter disillusionment after 1850, withdrew from commitments, and turned to social conservatism.

———. *George Ripley: Transcendentalist and Utopian Socialist.* Athens: University of Georgia Press, 1967. While the footnotes are sometimes unreliable, this biography offers a wealth of detail pertaining to Ripley's life and times prior to his New York years.

CURTIS, EDITH ROELKER. *A Season in Utopia: the Story of Brook Farm.* New York: Nelson, 1961. Bibliography offers the most complete listing of significant material published on Brook Farm from 1842 to 1956with the sole exception of John Sears' book.

DALL, CAROLINE HEALY. *Margaret and Her Friends, or Ten Conversations with Margaret Fuller.* Boston: Roberts, 1897. Describes Sophia Ripley as a Buddhist and Ripley as a Platonist who "seemed to be more conscious of the movement of the world than any of our party."

———. *Transcendentalism in New England.* Boston: Roberts, 1897. Credits Ripley's Brook Farm as chiefly responsible for arousing enthusiasm and for the continuing interest in Transcendentalism.

DANA, RICHARD HENRY, JR. *An Autobiographical Sketch.* Hamden: Shoestring Press, 1953. Tells of his studies with Ripley in 1823.

DUFFY, JOHN J, "Transcendental Letters from George Ripley to James Marsh." *Emerson Society Quarterly,* L (1968), 20-24.

EMERSON, RALPH WALDO. *The Complete Works of Ralph Waldo Emerson.* Edited by Edward Waldo Emerson. Boston: Houghton Mifflin, 1903-04.

———. *Journals of Ralph Waldo Emerson.* Edited by Edward Emerson and Waldo Emerson Forbes. Boston: Houghton Mifflin, 1909.

———. *The Letters of Ralph Waldo Emerson.* Edited by Ralph L. Rusk. New York: Columbia University Press, 1939.

FAUST, C. H. "The Background of the Unitarian Opposition to Transcendentalism," *Modern Philology,* XXXV (February, 1938), 297-324. Caught between the conservatism of Calvinism and the radicalism of the Transcendentalists, these Unitarian liberals are depicted in a sympathetic light.

FROTHINGHAM, OCTAVIUS BROOKS. *George Ripley.* Boston: Houghton Mifflin, 1882. Superficial but interesting biography; main virtue is that about half the text is composed of Ripley's own writings.

———. *Transcendentalism in New England.* New York: Putnam, 1876. Impressive history of Transcendentalism as seen by an intimate of Ripley's.

HAWTHORNE, NATHANIEL. *The Blithedale Romance.* New York: Modern Library, 1937. Fictional account of Brook Farm published in 1852. Not a faithful portrayal of Brook Farm or its members, the book does convey Hawthorne's ambiguous attitude toward reform and idealism.

ISELY, JETER and ELIZABETH. "A Note on George Ripley and the Beginnings of New England Transcendentalism," *Unitarian Historical Society Proceedings,* XIII (1961), 75-85. Gives more than usual credit to Ripley for his role in crystallizing the Transcendental movement in its initial stages.

KERN, ALEXANDER. "The Rise of Transcendentalism." *Transitions in American Literary History.* Durham: University of North Carolina Press, 1953. An intelligent chapter which does not simplify the complexities of Transcendentalism.

KINOY, ARTHUR. *"Arise and Depart, For This is not Your Rest": A Study of the Resignation of George Ripley.* Bowdoin Prize Essay, Harvard University, April 1, 1941. Explains link between Ripley's ministerial and Brook Farm goals.

KIRBY, GEORGIANA BRUCE. *Years of Experience.* New York: American Missionary Society Press, 1971. First published in 1887, this account by a woman who rose from servant to schoolteacher through her opportunity at Brook Farm gives many details and incidents that intellectuals and children of rich businessmen missed.

MOTT, FRANK L. *A History of American Magazines.* Cambridge: Harvard University Press, 1957. Summaries of staff, content, objectives, and publishing details of American magazines.

MYERSON, JOEL. "A Calendar of Transcendental Club Meetings," *American Literature,* XLIV (May, 1972), 197-207. Long-needed definitive record of the beginnings, activities, and membership of the club.

RILEY, WOODBRIDGE I. *American Thought from Puritanism to Pragmatism.* Gloucester: Henry Holt, 1915, 1959. Casual but suggestive description of Ripley's philosophy.

———. "Two Types of Transcendentalism in America." *Journal of Philosophy,* XV (May 23, 1918), 281-92. Argues that the roots of American Transcendentalism were already established before the importation of German and French thought.

RITTENHOUSE, CAROLINE SMITH. "The Testimony of Man's Inward Nature: A Study of George Ripley's Transcendentalism." Unpublished doctoral dissertation, Harvard, June, 1965. Exhaustive study of Ripley's philosophy and writings from 1830 to 1840.

RYCKMAN, LEWIS. "Address to the Working Men of New England." *The Harbinger,* I (1845), 21-22. A Brook Farmer as union organizer.

SCHULTZ, ARTHUR R., and HENRY A. POCHMANN. "George Ripley: Unitarian, Transcendentalist, or Infidel?" *American Literature,* XIV (March, 1942), 1-19. Article claims that Parker was more theologically radical than Ripley and that Ripley's mental growth stopped with the end of Brook Farm. A fine example of what egregious errors superb scholars can make when they trust too much to secondary source materials.

SEARS, JOHN VAN DER ZEE. *My Friends at Brook Farm.* New York: Desmond, FitzGerald, 1912. One of the most enjoyable personal accounts of Brook Farm life.

SLATER, JOSEPH. "George Ripley and Thomas Carlyle." *Publications of the Modern Language Association,* LXVII (June, 1952), 341-49. Most complete description to date of the relationship between Ripley, Emerson, and Carlyle.

THOMPSON, CAMERON. "John Locke and New England Transcendentalism." *New England Quarterly,* XXXV (1962), 435-57. Argues that Francis Bowen's two essays on Locke should be considered part of the Norton-Ripley controversy.

WELLECK, RENÉ. "The Minor Transcendentalists and German Philosophy." *New England Quarterly,* XV (1942), 652-80. Dated discussion of continental influences on American Transcendentalists, especially on Margaret Fuller and Ripley. Concludes without support that Ripley was more timid and more orthodox than Parker, the general appraisal of Ripley in the 1940's.

WILSON, HOWARD AARON. "George Ripley: Social and Literary Critic." Unpublished doctoral dissertation, University of Wisconsin, 1941. Wilson is one of the few critics to see Ripley's career as all of one piece. Emphasizes the latter part of his life.

Index

(The works of Ripley are listed under his name)